Unleashing
the
Potential
of the
Teenage
Brain

Unleashing
the
Potential
of the
Teenage
Brain

10 Powerful Ideas

Barry Corbin

CORWIN PRESS
A SAGE Publications Company
Thousand Oaks, CA 91320

For information:

Corwin Press
A Sage Publications Company
2455 Teller Road
Thousand Oaks, California 91320
www.corwinpress.com

Sage Publications Ltd.
1 Oliver's Yard
55 City Road
London, EC1Y 1SP
United Kingdom

Sage Publications India Pvt. Ltd.
B 1/I 1 Mohan Cooperative Industrial
    Area
Mathura Road, New Delhi 110 044
India

Sage Publications Asia-Pacific Pte. Ltd.
33 Pekin Street #02–01
Far East Square
Singapore 048763

Printed in the United States of America.

Library of Congress Cataloging-in-Publication Data

Corbin, Barry, 1946-
Unleashing the potential of the teenage brain : ten powerful ideas / Barry Corbin.
    p. cm.
Includes bibliographical references and index.
ISBN 978-1-4129-5762-5 (cloth)
ISBN 978-1-4129-4249-2 (pbk.)
    1. Learning, Psychology of. 2. Adolescents—Education. 3. Effective teaching.
4. Adolescent psychology. 5. Brain—Growth. I. Title.

LB1060.C6598 2008
370.15′23—dc22   2007011188

This book is printed on acid-free paper.

07   08   09   10   11   10   9   8   7   6   5   4   3   2   1

Acquisitions Editor:	Carol Chambers Collins
Editorial Assistant:	Gem Rabanera
Production Editor:	Veronica Stapleton
Copy Editor:	Renee Willers
Typesetter:	C&M Digitals (P) Ltd.
Proofreader:	Tracy Marcynzsyn
Indexer:	Rick Hurd
Cover Designer:	Lisa Miller
Graphic Designer:	Lisa Riley

Contents

Acknowledgments

T his text really had its beginning in 1999 when I and my fellow program consultant and professional colleague, Sue Lebel, attended the National School Conference Institute (NSCI) conference in Phoenix, Arizona titled, Assessment and Instruction: Infusing Brain Research, Multi-Intelligences, Learning Styles, and Mind Styles. This highly informative conference featured many of the prominent educators like Geoffrey and Renate Caine, Robert Sylwester, David Sousa, and Susan Kovalik, who were writing on the importance and relevance of brain research to teaching and learning. For both of us, this conference was an epiphany of sorts. We resolved to include much of what we had learned into professional development workshops for the nearly 1200 teachers and 45 schools for whom we had staff development responsibilities. In succeeding years, I was equally fortunate to attend other conferences where I became acquainted with the important work of writers such as Eric Jensen, Patricia Wolfe, Martha Kaufeldt, and others. Brain research and its application to the classroom became one of the major components of my own educational research as well as the key element of the professional workshops that I presented and facilitated.

During the last several years of my employment with the Annapolis Valley Region School Board (AVRSB), I was responsible for researching and developing alternative educational programs and transitional pathways for underachieving high school students. This experience, coupled with my nearly 20 years of teaching at the middle and high school levels, caused me to seriously rethink and doubt many of our traditional approaches to teaching adolescents. Conversations with many of these at-risk and underachieving students as well as those who find success in school made me realize that many of our current practices and approaches are inappropriate, misdirected, and ineffective. It seemed to me that we needed to look at the emerging research from neuroscience to see if there was something different about teenagers and their ways of thinking to find some better ways of teaching. Indeed the past 10 years or so of brain research has shown that there are very significant changes happening in the teenage brain and that there are truly better ways of reaching those adolescent brains—hence the focus of this book.

My thanks goes to my friend and colleague Sue who was along for most of this journey and to all the other consultants of the AVRSB who joined us later and whose ideas, conversations, and encouragement were always valued.

Special thanks must go to the countless numbers of teenagers I have taught and who have shown me what works and what does not work. Particular gratitude is extended to those students I met during my role as alternate programming consultant and who told me in very plain terms what is wrong with traditional high schools and conventional high school teaching. To the many teachers who attended my workshops and who offered sincere advice and constructive feedback, I also extend my thanks.

To Eric Jensen and the Brain Store who first supported and encouraged the concept for this book and to the editing staff at Corwin Press—in particular, Gem Rabanera—I offer my most sincere gratitude.

Finally, but most important, my wholehearted appreciation goes to my best friend and wife Ann, who always believes in me and that I am capable of accomplishing anything to which I put my mind.

Corwin Press thanks the following reviewers for their contributions to this book:

David Brock, AP Biology Instructor, Roland Park Country School, Baltimore, MD

Kathy Tritz-Rhodes, Teacher, Marcus-Meriden-Cleghorn Schools, Marcus, IA

Eric Kincaid, Teacher, Morgantown High School, Morgantown, WV

Mary Little, Associate Professor, University of Central Florida

Patricia Tucker, Regional Superintendent, DC Public Schools, Washington, DC

About the Author

Barry Corbin, MEd, is an educational consultant and part-time lecturer in the School of Education, Acadia University, Nova Scotia, Canada. Barry holds a Bachelor of Science degree (geology) from Acadia University, a Bachelor of Education from the same institution, and a Master of Education in curriculum development from St. Mary's University in Halifax, Nova Scotia. He is recently retired from the Annapolis Valley Regional School Board (AVRSB) where he served for over 30 years as teacher, school administrator, curriculum and program consultant, and staff developer. Barry has also served as consultant and advisor to several Department of Education initiatives for the province of Nova Scotia, Canada. In his last role with the AVRSB, he served as a youth pathways and transitions consultant where he was responsible for researching and developing alternate educational programs and pathways for underachieving high school students. As an independent consultant, he frequently presents at professional development workshops and inservices on such topics as brain-compatible teaching and learning, multiple intelligences and learning styles, differentiated instruction, authentic assessment, and collaborative and cooperative teaching strategies. His workshops are enthusiastically endorsed by those in attendance because he engages his audiences with many of the interactive strategies he advocates in his writing.

PART I

Discovering the Teenage Brain

1

Introduction: The Creatures in the Classroom!

Those Exasperating and Unfathomable Teenagers

HOW DO WE REACH AND TEACH THOSE UNPREDICTABLE TEENAGE BRAINS?

This book was written especially for those of us who work with, live with, teach, and otherwise associate with teenagers. Although it is primarily intended for secondary educators, it will also be extremely informative, helpful, and useful for parents of teenagers. Parents and secondary school teachers are equally familiar with those frustrating, unfathomable, exasperating, and sometimes downright bizarre individuals called teenagers: that sweet, quiet, well-dressed girl who now is noticeably outspoken and dyes her hair pink and dresses in all black; that surly young man who dozes on a desk at the back of the room and dares you to confront him; another girl who is on an emotional roller coaster from day to day; that perplexing young man who was at the top of the class in elementary school, but who now barely does enough to get by; that young lady who you always thought exercised sound judgment, but who was arrested for drunk driving this past weekend; and all those dozens of odd characters who just do not seem to care about school and what you are teaching. It is a strange thing, the teenage brain. It is hard to figure out what they are thinking or if, indeed, they are thinking at all. Then suddenly, miraculously at about 18 or 19, they start to make some sensible decisions and show some insight and consideration for others. Adolescence is such a confused and confusing time for parents, teachers, and, most of all, for the teenagers themselves. You have always thought that there must be some strange, surprising, and unexplained things going on in their brains. It turns out that you were right! But knowing this, how does that help us unlock that tremendous potential that we know lies in the brain of every one of those unpredictable individuals?

WANTED: A NEW APPROACH TO TEACHING TEENAGERS!

As recently as the 1990s, many professionals—psychologists, educators, and, indeed, neuroscientists—thought that the brain essentially stopped growing and developing by the age of five or six years and that the teenage brain was virtually the same as the adult brain and could think and function in the same way. It was only those pesky hormones that caused such erratic and irrational behavior in teenagers! However, more recent neuroscientific research suggests that the teenage brain is undergoing tremendous changes during adolescence and that the teenage years may be one of the most vital times for brain development. It appears that, more than ever, it is crucial that we find ways of effectively teaching teenagers and of maximizing the growth potential in their surprisingly different and dynamic brains.

> The teenage years may be one of the most vital times for brain development!

Regrettably many, if not most, secondary school teachers are unaware of this research and the numerous other findings about the brain and how it learns. Or if they are, they often fail to see the implications for their classrooms and their teaching; or perhaps, they do not know how to translate this important information about teaching and learning into practical and effective classroom strategies. Even very successful teachers often are not able to make the pedagogical connections between the effective teaching strategies and activities that they are using and the possible cognitive and neurological reasons for this success. Of greater concern is that many teachers and schools continue to use approaches and methods that are decidedly incompatible with how we now know the brain actually learns; and worse, these methods are quite ineffective for most of the students they are teaching. Often teachers persist in using methodologies that they feel more comfortable with or have gotten some good results with in the past. In many cases, teachers will admit that they know relatively little about the new ideas, theories, and approaches to teaching and learning and dismiss these new ideas as fads, bandwagons, or lacking credibility. Under the considerable pressure of getting better results with students and faced with greater and greater calls for teacher and school accountability, teachers and schools are often fearful that experimenting with other approaches and methods will further erode what successes they have experienced. Politicians and numerous other "educational experts" persist in asking teachers to administer more of the same, certain that we will be able to "cure" our students despite considerable evidence to the contrary.

What we need is a more scientific approach to teaching and learning—an approach in which teachers come to recognize the implications of the considerable research on the brain and how this enhanced understanding of the brain and the ways that it learns impacts what we should be doing in the classroom. In the past two decades, there have been many advances in our understanding of the human brain and the learning process. Within the past several years, this has been particularly true for the teenage brain. Many of the views long held by psychologists and neuroscientists about adolescence, the teen brain, and its capacity to learn are being challenged and overturned by these new research findings. Through this enhanced understanding and knowledge, a number of educators and teachers are beginning to discover and implement teaching strategies and pedagogical approaches that are more compatible with how the brain actually learns, making teaching and learning considerably more effective. However, because many secondary teachers were trained prior to these advances and have had little opportunity to research and learn about these exciting brain-compatible strategies and approaches, they continue to use the more traditional methodologies and become increasingly frustrated with the results. Daniels, Bizar, and Zemelman (2001) have observed that high schools, and indeed most middle schools and junior highs, are notoriously resistant to change, and it is often difficult to convince teachers and schools to try other approaches. Undoubtedly our understanding of the human brain will further evolve with more and more research in this area. Thus we would expect that there would be even greater understanding of the teenage brain and the learning process. This new knowledge will enable us to design teaching strategies and pedagogical approaches to take advantage of the way that the learning occurs naturally and in ways that are most compatible with the brain. This is the focus of this book, to provide an introductory look at what we presently know about the human brain—particularly, the teenage brain—and learning and how we might, as classroom teachers, extend this knowledge into effective brain-compatible teaching and learning. It is intended to be a practical hands-on, how-to book providing both a synopsis of the current research in a number of areas of brain research and learning theory and, more important, also matching the theory with the implications for teaching and learning by providing numerous examples of practical effective in-class brain-compatible strategies.

WHY EDUCATORS NEED TO LEARN ABOUT THE TEENAGE BRAIN

"The most surprising thing (about looking at the adolescent brain) has been how much the teen brain is changing."

Jay Giedd, interviewed in Frontline:
Inside the Teenage Brain, 2002

"The more we understand the brain, the better we'll be able to design instruction to match how it learns best."

Patricia Wolfe, Brain Matters:
Translating Research Into Classroom Practice, 2001, p. 2

All teachers want to become more effective at what they do. It is only by examining their own teaching practices, strategies, and techniques and the philosophical, theoretical, and scientific basis for these practices that they can hope to improve and build upon what they know works well with students. Effective teaching practice must be grounded in sound research about learning and what constitutes effective teaching.

Since all teachers seek to become more effective at what they do, it makes good sense for them to know something about the organ that they are trying to affect—that is, the brain. Teaching, in a sense, is about changing the brain every day in the classroom. We are coming to recognize that this is dramatically most true for those who teach teenagers. In much the same way that a mechanic needs to know about the functioning of an automobile, or the computer technician about the computer, teachers can do much more effective jobs if they know something about the structure of the brain, how it is developing, how it functions, and how it learns. With this knowledge, they are more likely to be able to organize teaching and utilize methodologies in ways that are most consistent with how the brain actually learns. By using this new information and understanding how the brain learns, teachers can develop teaching strategies and learning activities that will make teaching and learning more effective, efficient, and enjoyable for both teacher and students. This is really what brain-compatible teaching is all about.

"If we agree that our schools are about learning, then shouldn't we be learning everything we can about what makes our brain thrive? School failures are not about bad schools, bad kids, or bad teachers; they're rather about the violation of the brain's basic operating principles."

Eric Jensen and Michael Dabney, Learning Smarter: The New Science of Teaching, 2000, pg xii

Teaching is an extremely challenging profession with more demands being placed on teachers every day. Teachers everywhere are looking for ways to make their own classroom practices more effective, efficient, and rewarding for both teachers and students. Regardless of how talented or innovative teachers are, often there is still some incompatibility or disconnect between what they are doing as teachers and how students actually learn. Brain-compatible teaching offers a way for teachers to reconcile this incompatibility and to close the gap between practice and theory. In short, the more we know as teachers about the brain and how it learns, the more effective we can become at helping all students learn.

BRAIN-COMPATIBLE TEACHING AND THE NEW SCIENCE OF LEARNING

The first reference to brain-compatible teaching is often traced to Leslie Hart's (1983, 1998) landmark text, *Human Brain and Human Learning*, in which he suggested that teaching and learning ought to be "brain-based" and matched with what he termed the true "nature of the brain" (p. xi). Borrowing from Hart's earlier definition, other writers have expanded upon this concept. Figure 1.1 summarizes how some of these writers have described brain-compatible teaching. Eric Jensen (1998a), who writes widely on the applications of brain research to teaching, cautions, however, that educators need to recognize that "brain-compatible learning theory is not a doctrine, nor is it a recipe to follow. Brain-compatible is, rather, a comprehensive approach to learning based on how neuroscience and cognitive research suggests the human brain best learns. And since the human brain is unique, there is no **one best** [bold added] way to do it," although there are some important principles and big ideas that ought to be recognized and followed (p. 37).

Figure 1.1   Four Definitions for Brain-Compatible Teaching

"Brain-based learning involves acknowledging the brain's rules for meaningful learning and organizing teaching with those rules in mind."

Caine and Caine (1994)

"A teaching environment which allows the brain to work as it naturally, and thus most powerfully, works."

Kovalik (1994)

"Brain-compatible teaching and learning are processes that parallel or complement the way the brain/mind makes meaning and remembers."

Fogarty (1997)

"Brain-compatible teaching is a research based, multidisciplinary approach to the question of how our brain best learns."

Jensen (1998a)

A New Science of Learning

In a 2004 report of the Organisation for Economic Co-operation and Development (Ball, 2001) summarizing the *OECD Second High Forum on Brain Mechanisms and Youth Learning*, Sir Christopher Ball proposed that a new "science of learning"(and teaching!) was emerging. Ball suggested that this new science of learning was needed to accurately reflect and represent the combined body of knowledge originating from the latest research in neuroscience and modern cognitive and learning theories integrated with the well-documented and effective pedagogical practices of successful teachers. He called for greater cooperation, better communication, and interdisciplinary work among educators, cognitive scientists, and neuroscientists. This interdisciplinary approach, he argued, would allow us to make well-researched evaluations about the effectiveness of certain teaching and learning strategies and would enable us to publicize and promote those brain-compatible strategies proven to be the most useful and effective. Scientists should be encouraged to share well-informed principles about the brain that are relevant to learning, and teachers should be invited to "share their knowledge among themselves and share this knowledge with the neuroscientific community" (Ball, 2001, p. 21). This, in turn, would enable the neuroscience community to "ground at least some of its research questions within the authentic experiences of good teachers" (Ball, 2001, p. 21). Ball maintains that we need to "move away from a learning system which is **curriculum-led** to a learning system which is **pedagogy-led** [bold added]" (p. 21). Further he says, "The pedagogy is more important than the curriculum. And yet across the world, we have educational services which are curriculum-led: that is not the way to create a 'brain-friendly' educational service" (p. 19).

[We need to] "move away from a learning system which is curriculum-led to a learning system which is pedagogy-led."

Christopher Ball, OECD Report on Second High Forum on Brain Mechanisms and Youth Learning, *2001, p. 19*

THE EMERGENCE OF A NEW PEDAGOGICAL MODEL

We might say that brain-compatible teaching and this new science of learning are really one in the same. In order to teach in the ways that the brain learns best, teachers need to draw upon this emerging science of learning. Using their knowledge and understanding of ideas, theories, and principles—which originate within the three fields of neuroscience, cognitive science, and educational psychology and research—teachers will come to realize the full benefits of a brain-compatible classroom. The intersection (see Figure 1.2) of these three components—neuroscience and brain research, cognitive theory, and educational psychology and theory—forms a pedagogical model that should be used as a foundation for teachers who wish to refine and transform their teaching strategies, practices, and approaches into ones that will maximize the learning opportunities for all types of learners in their classrooms—a learning system that is pedagogy-led.

Figure 1.2   A New Pedagogical Model

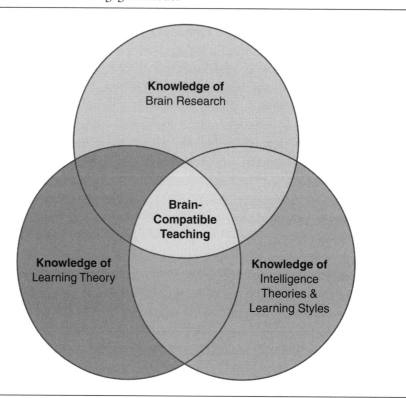

The chief focus of this book is to provide an introductory look at this new pedagogical model, examining what we know about research on the human brain (in particular, the adolescent brain), the integration of this brain research with learning theory and ideas about intelligence, and how this influences and relates to effective teaching. It is also hoped that teachers will be able to immediately apply this new understanding by referencing numerous examples of practical and timely applications of brain-compatible strategies and approaches included within the text.

2

Adolescence and the Teenage Brain

What Is Different and
How Do We Know?

ADOLESCENCE—JUST THE QUICK FACTS!

"Adolescence is an extremely sensitive period from a brain perspective, and also due to a surge of hormones in the body. It is a period when children are especially open to social development, but less open to learning at school, and it is also a time when violent behaviour [sic] usually starts. Although there is a vast amount of cognitive research on adolescence, there is not much available from neuroscience and this gap needs to be bridged."

OECD Full Report on Emotions and
Learning and Education: Forum on
Brain and Learning, *December 2004, p. 13*

Adolescence generally refers to the period of transition from childhood and dependence to adulthood and independence. Often it has no really discernible beginning or end, but it approximately covers the period of 11–20 years of age. As one might surmise, there is considerable variability among teenagers in terms of the changes that occur during this time period and the pace at which these changes take place. Girls tend to experience these changes at an earlier age than boys. It is wise to remember as well that adolescence is a fairly long period and that it can be seen to have different stages or phases within this time period as the child moves gradually and progressively from childhood to adulthood. Generally, however, adolescence is characterized by these changes (Figure 2.1).

Figure 2.1   Major Changes During the Adolescent Years

1. Rapid physical changes and growth:

   Significant and rapid gains in height and weight

   Appearance and maturation of secondary sexual characteristics

   Changes in sleeping, eating habits, and energy levels

   Stages of awkwardness and clumsiness due to growth spurts

   Continued brain development

2. Changes in cognitive and intellectual development:

   Development and improvement in reasoning, problem-solving, and abstract-thinking skills

   Development of ability to reflect upon one's thinking and learning (i.e., metacognition)

   Increase in range of intellectual interests

   Heightened sense of self-consciousness

3. Changes in sexuality:

   Need to establish sexual identity and become comfortable with one's own sexuality

   Increased interest in sexual matters and need to establish sense of intimacy

   Concerns with normal physical development and attractiveness to others

   Experimentation with sexual activities and relationships

4. Social and emotional changes:

   High focus on one's self—teens often believe that nearly everyone around them is watching them and is as concerned with their thoughts and behaviors as they are

   Strong desire to be with peers—peer group often influences interests and choices

   Resistance to directions and advice from authority figures

   Need to establish identity, autonomy, and sense of belonging—often struggles with sense of identity

(Continued)

Figure 2.1 (Continued)

Increased risk-taking and experimentation—teens often have a sense of indestructibility and belief that it cannot happen to me

Increased development of values, morals, and sense of conscience

Increased ability to express emotions and to communicate more effectively

Moodiness, rapid emotional changes—particularly in early adolescence

Need to establish a sense of value and achievement—development of stronger work ethic (sense of pride in one's work)

Gradual move to self-reliance, independence, and ability to self-regulate self esteem

Note: The above summaries are compiled from information available from the Web sites of National Library of Medicine and Institute of Health, www.nlm.nih.gov; the Virginia Cooperative Extension, www.ext.vt.edu; and the American Academy of Child and Adolescent Psychiatry, www.aacap.org

THE TEENAGE BRAIN— WHAT WE HAD BELIEVED

> Our previous ideas about the teenage brain and how it functions now appear to be quite inaccurate.

Up until recently (as recent as the mid 1990s), neuroscientists, psychologists, and teachers had, we now believe, an inaccurate picture of the teenage brain and how it functions. Now, chiefly through the advances of medical imaging technology, we are discovering some quite surprising and revealing things about the teenage brain. However, prior to this new understanding, what was generally believed to be true for the teenage brain and adolescent behavior can be summarized in Figure 2.2.

Figure 2.2   What We Used To Believe About the Teen Brain

Most brain growth and development took place in the womb and in the few years shortly after birth. Because the brain was already 95% of the size of the adult brain by age 5 or 6, most brain development and organization was already in place at this time. The rest of the developing and growing was finished by the age of 12 years.

Because the brain was full grown in size at about age 12, many psychologists felt that teens were capable of the highest stages of cognitive processing and thinking at this time. Because their brains were essentially the same size, teenagers could and should think like adults.

The often erratic and irrational behavior and poor decision making during the teen years could be attributed to peer pressure, societal influences, and the tremendous flood of hormonal changes during puberty.

It is normal and natural social development for teens to direct their emotions at and rebel against parents and authority figures because it is just their efforts to define who they are and to test out and assert their independence.

HOW NEUROSCIENCE AND MEDICAL TECHNOLOGY ARE CHANGING OUR IDEAS ABOUT THE TEENAGE BRAIN

"Imaging techniques have provided a revolutionary new view into how the activation of neural circuits in the brain give rise to mental processes such as memory, emotion, decision-making and reasoning."

Daniel Siegel, interview in Frontline:
Inside the Teenage Brain, 2002

As recently as several decades ago, the only ways that neuroscientists had to study and observe the brain in action were highly invasive, medically risky, and could generally show only some sketchy aspects about the exterior surface of the brain (i.e., the part you see when you open up the skull). The main way that neuroscientists could observe brain anatomy in detail, particularly its internal structures, was through dissection after death. This, of course, told them little about the functioning and purposes of the different areas of the brain. Today, however, hardly a week goes by that we do not hear about some new, exciting, and potentially revealing research from neuroscience about the brain and how it functions. These rapid and revealing discoveries can be attributed to tremendous advances (beginning in the early 1970s) in medical technology, particularly in computer assisted imaging technology, which provides neuroscientists with extremely detailed images of the living brain while it is actually functioning and processing information. Figure 2.3 summarizes some of the most useful technologies that have led to many surprising and revealing discoveries about the brain and how it functions.

Figure 2.3   Important Developments in Neuroscience Technology

Technology and Approximate Time of First Use	Function and Type of Information It Can Provide
EEG (Electroencephalograph; 1940s)	First noninvasive method to allow neuroscientists to measure brain activity. Measures electrical signals generated by brain activity and can give scientists information about brain activity over a period of time and connections between different parts of the brain.
CAT or CT (Computerized axial tomography; early 1970s)	A scanning and imaging procedure that uses many two-dimensional X-ray images of the brain to produce cross-sections through the brain. Particularly useful in detecting damage in certain areas of brain and small changes in cerebral blood flow.
PET (Positron emission tomography; mid 1970s)	Allows scientists to observe blood flow or metabolism in any part of the brain using radioactively tagged glucose injected into blood stream. Allows scientists to see more active areas of the brain and fairly deep structures within the brain.
MRI (Magnetic resonance imaging; 1977)	Uses powerful magnetic field and radio wave pulses to create very precise three-dimensional pictures of the brain.
fMRI (Functional magnetic resonance imaging; 1992)	Fairly recent advance in scanning technology. Can map out precisely where brain activity is taking place, and to what degree, in real time by measuring variations in amount of oxygen brain cells are consuming.
MEG (Magneto-encephalography; late 1990s to 2000)	Very recent neuroscience technology that is quite rare due to its large size and high costs. Can give scientists the most detailed and accurate picture of neuron activity in real time.

THE FUTURE OF BRAIN IMAGING

The neuroscience newsletter issue of *BrainWork* focusing on neuroimaging points out that new and more sophisticated neural imaging techniques are being developed very rapidly; and within the near future, brain scanning technology may be able to identify brain functioning right down to the level of synaptic connections (Patoine, 2005). Today, through the integration of research from mathematics, computer science, and neuroscience, there are greater and even greater applications of complex computer analysis to the information received through various scanning techniques. According to Arthur Toga, head of the Laboratory of Neuro Imaging at the University of

California at Los Angeles, this allows neuroscientists to gain "a much more comprehensive view of what's happening in a normal brain and what's going wrong in pathological conditions" (cited in Patoine, 2005, p. 3). What is most exciting is the increasing ability of neuroscientists to see the brain in real time. Because most brain functioning occurs in less than a second or two, this greater ability to measure what is happening in faster times coupled with cellular studies and the new field of optical two-photon imaging is certain to give us more comprehensive views of the brain and how it functions.

3

Big Changes in the Teenage Brain

What We Have Learned and Are Learning

THE TEENAGE BRAIN—A WORK IN PROGRESS

"Teenagers' brains are not broken; they're just still under construction."

Jay Giedd, cited in "Brain Immaturity Can Be Deadly" by Elizabeth Williamson, 2005, p. 3

The human brain is a watery gelatinous mass of nerve and supporting tissue located in the human skull and connected to the rest of the body's nervous system through the spinal cord. The adult brain weighs about 1400 grams (1.4 kg) and is the approximate size of two human fists placed side to side. Human brains consist of three major parts: the *brain stem*, the *cerebellum*, and the *cerebrum*. There are also a number of other smaller specialized structures and other primitive cell areas that suggest the earlier evolutionary stages of the brain (the so called reptilian brain). The brain is subdivided into two distinct sides (the left and right hemispheres) joined by a thick bundle of nerve fibers called the *corpus callosum*. Until quite recently, neuroscientists believed that the brain was primarily finished growing and developing by the time we were five or six years old. Most of the growth appeared to have happened prior to birth; and by age six, the brain was 90% to 95% of adult size. The prevalent view was that the rest of the development took place very slowly during childhood; and by adolescence, our brains were essentially adult size. Today we know that is not the case. Neuroscientists have discovered that surprising, dramatic, and significant changes are happening in the teenage brain. So dramatic and significant, that many researchers describe the adolescent brain as a work in progress.

FROM BACK TO FRONT:

> Surprising, dramatic, and significant changes are happening in the teenage brain.

BRAIN GROWTH, NEURON PROLIFERATION AND PRUNING, MYELIN DEVELOPMENT

The functional and information processing parts of the brain (the cerebral cortex) are composed of two main types of material—gray matter and white matter. The gray matter is made of brain nerve cells called neurons. There may be as many as 100 billion neurons in the brain. Neurons differ from other cells in the human body in that they do not appear to be able to regenerate but are able to transmit or communicate information to other neurons through electrochemical signals. Most neurons are composed of three main parts: the body cell containing the nucleus, thousands of tiny fingerlike projections called *dendrites*, and a single arm or fiber called the *axon*.

The white matter of the brain is called *myelin*. Myelin is a white fatty substance that covers the axon in a nerve cell like a sheath. It insulates the axon, allowing electrical impulses to pass more quickly and without interruption. Neuroscientists believe that we are born with most of the neurons that we will ever have, but that new experiences and learning create more connections (called *synapses*) and neural pathways among these neurons as the brain processes new sensory information.

The greatest density of brain cells actually occurs in the womb where an overproduction of neurons takes place around the third to sixth month of gestation. However just prior to birth, a process called *pruning* takes place in which many unnecessary brain cells are eliminated. Between the age of 5 or 6 and the onset of puberty, neurons grow many more of these dendrites, forming dozens of new connections to other neurons and creating many new pathways for neuron signals. This appears to peak at about age 11 or 12. Recently, neuroscientific research has shown us that a second dramatic stage of neuron proliferation and pruning takes place during the adolescent years with the most critical part of this process (the one affecting the highest mental functions) occurring during the late teens. The average teenager appears to lose about 15% of excess gray matter. The trigger for this second phase of proliferation and pruning may be the great surge of sex hormones at the onset of puberty. During this time, the number of neurons does not actually change significantly, but the number of connections (synapses) between neurons is greatly increased and thousands of new neural pathways may be formed. However, during adolescence, most of these new neural pathways will be pruned away depending on whether they are used or not. Neural pathways that are reinforced by frequent use will be strengthened and maintained while those that are not will be lost due to pruning. Puberty is marked by this dramatic increase in neuron connectivity and growth throughout many parts of the brain. Throughout the adolescent years, this growth and development proceeds in stages (really fits and spurts!) from the back of the brain to the front. Those parts of the brain reaching maturity earliest are in the back of the brain while the last areas to develop fully are in the front of the brain—the *prefrontal cortex*.

Changes are also happening in the myelin—the white matter of the brain.

> Puberty is marked by a dramatic increase in neuron connectivity and growth throughout many parts of the brain.

There is a noticeable late maturation of this *myelination* process in the frontal cortex of adolescents. Myelin development around neurons appears to progressively thicken from birth to adulthood with a noticeable subsiding during adolescence. Increased myelination implies more mature and efficient neuron connections. As neuron pruning takes place, one notices thicker, and thus better, myelin insulation around neuron cells. Just as insulation improves the conductivity of electrical wires, this thickening of myelin makes nerve transmission faster and more efficient, creating greater efficiency in that part of the brain. Jay Giedd (cited in Wallis, 2004) points out that these two processes—neuron pruning and myelin thickening—results in fewer but faster connections in the brain. However, this increased myelination in the teenage brain also has some unfortunate consequences. After neurons have become completely myelinated, they are more rigid and less able to establish new neural pathways. This means some of the great potential for learning and accepting new experiences that once lay in the developing teenage brain is now lost forever.

> During adolescence, many neural pathways will be pruned away because the pathways are not used.

Figure 3.1   Dynamic and Surprising Changes Inside the Teenage Brain

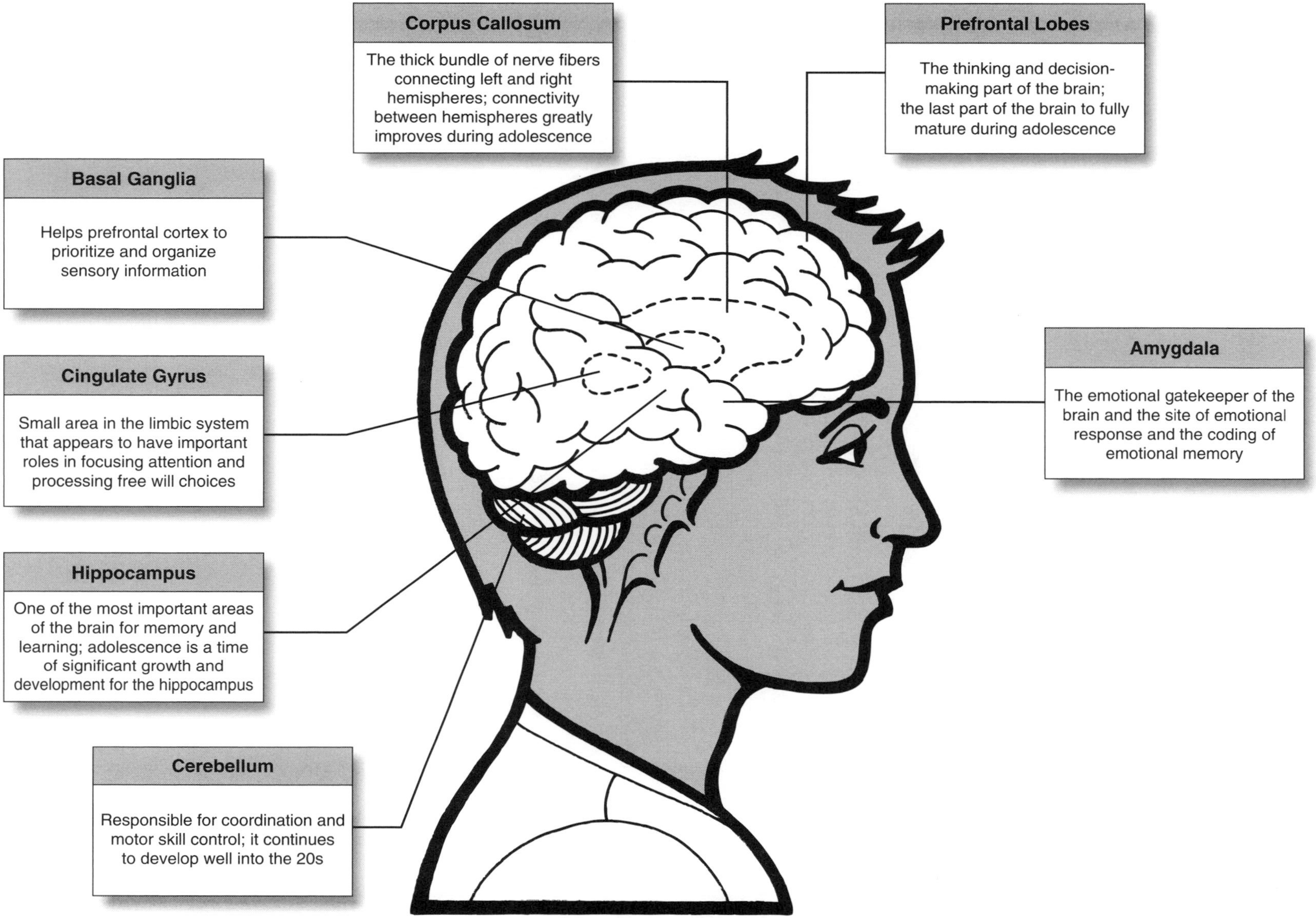

Prefrontal Lobes

The thinking and decision-making part of the brain; the last part of the brain to fully mature during adolescence

Amygdala

The emotional gatekeeper of the brain and the site of emotional response and the coding of emotional memory

Corpus Callosum

The thick bundle of nerve fibers connecting left and right hemispheres; connectivity between hemispheres greatly improves during adolescence

Basal Ganglia

Helps prefrontal cortex to prioritize and organize sensory information

Cingulate Gyrus

Small area in the limbic system that appears to have important roles in focusing attention and processing free will choices

Hippocampus

One of the most important areas of the brain for memory and learning; adolescence is a time of significant growth and development for the hippocampus

Cerebellum

Responsible for coordination and motor skill control; it continues to develop well into the 20s

The Prefrontal Cortex

The prefrontal cortex is frequently referred to as the executive center of the brain because this is the area of the brain that plays an important role in rational thought, planning, organization, decision making, problem solving, and cognitive processing. The prefrontal cortex is part of the larger cerebral cortex or *neocortex*, which refers to the thin (about 1 mm to 7 or 8 mm thick) wrinkled skinlike outer layer covering the cerebrum, the largest part of the brain. This layer is the so called gray matter of the brain and is the part of the brain where such processes as cognition, problem solving, language, and vision take place. The neocortex, and thus the cerebrum, is subdivided into four major areas or lobes: the frontal lobes, the occipital lobes, the temporal lobes, and the parietal lobes. Each lobe or area is responsible for processing different sensory information and memory connections.

> The prefrontal cortex—the thinking and decision-making part of the brain—is the last part to fully mature during adolescence.

The prefrontal cortex is found at the top and front of the brain just behind the forehead. It is this area that essentially makes us human, allowing us to be consciously aware of our actions and their consequences. Neuroscientists have discovered that the prefrontal cortex is the last part of the brain to fully mature during adolescence and that there is evidence that this part of the brain continues to develop well into the mid-twenties. It appears to grow somewhat during the preteen years and then decrease slightly in size during the teen years as neural connections and pathways are pruned and consolidated during this time.

The Cerebellum

> Research has shown dramatic changes in the cerebellum during adolescence.

The cerebellum is one of the three major parts of the brain. Located just behind the brain stem at the rear and base of the brain, it is mainly responsible for controlling basic muscle movements and motor skills as well as such functions as the coordination of balance and body posture. Neuroscientists feel it may also help regulate certain higher-level thought processes such as mathematical reasoning, advanced social interaction, decision-making capabilities, and the prioritizing of emotional information. The cerebellum appears to be the only part of the brain that continues to grow well into the twenties. Research has shown dramatic changes in the cerebellum during adolescence. There are significant increases in the growth of neurons and the development of neural pathways and connections. Because coordination and motor skill control is so closely tied to the cerebellum, these dramatic changes in the cerebellum during adolescence may explain the bouts of clumsiness and lack of physical coordination that teenagers frequently experience during early adolescence.

The Limbic System

The *limbic system* is sometimes referred to as the primitive brain because it includes some of the earliest structures in the brain's evolution. It is a group of various connected structures of the brain that deal with emotional response and control. It also influences such aspects as hunger, thirst, sleep, sexual response, and hormone production. The limbic system includes the *amygdala, basal ganglia, hippocampus, hypothalamus,* and an area called the *cingulate gyrus*. The limbic system is particularly affected by the great surge of sex hormones produced during adolescence. Various neurotransmitters (brain chemicals) that control and regulate such things as mood, impulse, motivation, and emotional excitability are greatly influenced by sex hormones produced during this emotionally explosive time in an individual's life. Because of this, teenagers often experience emotional highs and lows more quickly and, at the same time, have less control over these emotions.

> Teenagers often experience emotional highs and lows more quickly than adults and have less control over these emotions.

The Basal Ganglia

The basal ganglia is a series of small structures located below the cerebral cortex. It is chiefly responsible for motor function (both small and large scale) and also helps the prefrontal cortex to prioritize and organize sensory information and make decisions. It seems to be closely connected to the prefrontal cortex as its development and maturation closely parallels that of the prefrontal cortex (Wallis, 2004).

The Cingulate Gyrus

The cingulated gyrus, part of the limbic system, is a small curved fold or ridge located between each brain hemisphere just above the corpus callosum. This small region, particularly the segment called the *anterior cingulate*, has become an area of special attention for neuroscientists because it is a part of the brain that appears to have important functions in focusing attention, regulating aggressive behavior, anticipating rewards, and processing free will choices (i.e., the ones we make when confronted with several alternatives rather than life-threatening decisions; Sylwester, 2003). The cingulate gyrus also appears to be "the main conduit between emotion and reward" (Smith, 2002, p. 60) and greatly affects motivation in learning. Research has shown that, like many parts of the brain, it is an area that is undergoing significant change and slow maturation during adolescence.

The Amygdala

The amygdala is a roughly almond-sized and -shaped structure (specialized group of cells) in the interior base of the brain. It is believed that the amygdala is the site of emotional response and is responsible for the coding of emotional memory. As such, it is sometimes referred to as the emotional gatekeeper for the brain. Functional magnetic resonance imaging (fMRI) scans show that teenagers rely more heavily on the amygdala when processing emotional information than do adults. As teenagers develop into adults, more of this decision making gets shifted to the more rational prefrontal lobe.

> Brain scans show that teenagers rely more heavily on the amygdala when processing emotional information than do adults.

The Corpus Callosum

The corpus callosum is a large thick bundle of nerve fibers that connect the left and right hemispheres of the brain, permitting communication between the two sides. During adolescence, there is a noticeable thickening of these nerve fibers connecting the two hemispheres (Wallis, 2004). Consequently, this greatly improves the ability of the brain to process information because of this higher conductivity between the two sides of the brain. Rapid communication between the two sides of the brain is particularly important in problem solving and creativity. For example, research (Davis, 2004) suggests that persons who are math-gifted are so because they can more efficiently utilize both sides of their brain during problem solving. Their brains apparently can communicate back and forth across the corpus callosum very quickly between the two hemispheres.

The Hippocampus

This is a small crescent-shaped structure in the interior of the brain. It appears to be one of the most important areas of the brain for memory processing and the formation of long-term memories. Like all areas of the brain during adolescence, it undergoes extensive pruning and neuron thickening during this time. Since it is so vital in the development of long-term memory, adolescence may be a particularly important time for its growth and development. This growth and development in the hippocampus during the teenage years is clearly affected by lots of diverse learning experiences and opportunities to form memories through many different neural pathways. Growth in the hippocampus has also been shown to be linked to and influenced by physical activity. Thus it appears to be essential for teenagers to engage in a variety of physical activities during these years in order to optimize the development of this vital part of the brain.

> Growth in the hippocampus has been shown to be linked to and influenced by physical activity.

The Pineal Gland

The *pineal gland* is a small endocrine organ in the interior of the brain. Its main function is to secrete the hormone *melatonin*, which regulates the sleep-awake cycle. Research has shown that during the adolescent years, the rate of melatonin production in the pineal gland changes. The result is that the sleep-awake cycle for teenagers is altered so that the brain's signal for shutting down for nighttime comes later in the day. Teenagers frequently find it difficult to go to sleep at the same evening times they had been accustomed to as preteens.

A Flood of Hormones

Neuroscientists and adolescent psychologists now largely discount the idea that the tremendous emotional upheaval in adolescents can be totally blamed on their hormonal levels. Nonetheless, the great flood of hormones during puberty still greatly affects the teenage brain. At the time of puberty, the sex glands as well as the adrenal glands begin to secrete high amounts of hormones like estrogen, testosterone, and other similar biochemicals into the blood stream. Recent neuroscience findings point out that these hormones are particularly active in the brain, influencing the production of other chemicals and neurotransmitters like serotonin and dopamine—chemicals which regulate emotions and stimulate mood and excitability. The limbic system (the emotional center of the brain) seems to be especially affected by these sex hormones.

WHAT IT ALL MEANS (WE THINK!)

A Word of Caution

Neuroscientists are always careful to offer a few words of caution about making bold claims concerning the relationship between brain imaging and human behavior and between emotion and learning. They often remind us that matching a particular area of activity in the brain, as seen on a brain scan, with a certain mental process does not necessarily mean that this is where the behavior or process originates. Frequently, the evidence supplied by neuroimaging must be substantiated and corroborated by other and additional neuroscience research and studies. For example, studies of persons with brain impairments and damage, sleep studies, or other types of cognitive and psychological research can often support findings identified through neuroimaging. Neuroscientists often warn us that neuroscience is such a new field that findings and facts discovered about the brain and its development just a few months ago are likely to be refuted and overturned as new information is learned. The danger is that educators and others can be overzealous in interpreting the significance and application of these exciting findings, particularly as it applies to teaching and the classroom. However, despite these caveats, there are many conclusions and findings from neuroscience research that can provide considerable guidance, practicality, and application to creating a more brain-compatible learning environment for the teenage brain.

Surprising and Significant Changes

Neuroscientists have discovered that there are numerous surprising and highly significant changes happening in the teenage brain. These discoveries are often quite dramatic and revealing about teenager behavior and their socio-emotional and intellectual development. Here are 12 of the most important discoveries:

1. A dynamic period of brain development, restructuring, and consolidation:

There is a dynamic period of brain development, restructuring, and consolidation during the teen years. This reorganization of the brain generally proceeds from back to front. As teenagers develop into adults, the overall focus of brain activity seems to shift from the emotional center of the brain (the limbic system) to areas of the brain (the prefrontal cortex) that influence and regulate self-control, rational decision making, problem solving, organization, and planning. Thus as teenagers progress through adolescence, their ability to utilize higher levels of cognitive processing and abstract thinking improves considerably and their reliance on emotionally based thinking and decision making lessens.

2. Maturation and development of cognitive functioning and higher-level thinking skills:

Cognitive neuron development and higher-level thinking skills continue to mature and develop well into the mid twenties. The prefrontal cortex is the last region of the teenage brain to undergo the myelination and hardwiring process associated with neuron thickening and pruning. Since this region of the brain is the area that plays a major role in decision making, rational thinking and planning, problem solving, organization, and other higher-level functions, teenagers (particularly early adolescents) have lower capacities for these mental processes than adults. Dr. Christiane Poulin, holder of the Canada Research Chair in population health and addictions research at Dalhousie University's medical school, reports that her research shows a noticeable change in the attitude of teenagers toward the possible harmful effects of drugs as they grow older (cited in Gillis, 2005). As a consequence, using "harm reduction" (see note below) approaches in drug education for a group of teenagers aged 12–15 does not seem to be particularly effective. In an article in *The Chronicle-Herald*, Poulin says, "We realized they simply did not have the maturity and the development to handle the complex decision-making that is required by harm reduction" whereas older students had the capacity to identify and recognize the problems and risks associated with substance abuse (cited in Gillis, 2005, p. B2). She concludes that "it would be best to teach teens aged 11 to 15 just to stay away from these drugs" rather than rely on their rational thinking about the harmful consequences of drug use (cited in Gillis, 2005, p. B2).

Note: Harm reduction is a strategy designed to acknowledge that if one can't prevent substance use or abuse, then you should be able to prevent some of the problems surrounding it by identifying these problems and risks and encouraging users to engage in less risky and harmful behaviors.

3. Control and regulation of novelty-seeking impulses:

Another one of the functions of the prefrontal cortex is to control and regulate the novelty seeking and natural curiosity impulses. Since the prefrontal cortex is maturing more slowly during adolescence, the teen brain's natural tendency for intrinsic curiosity is often low at this time. Consequently, teens often require more immediate extrinsic or external motivators than adults might need to become interested in a learning task. On the other hand, the impulse inhibition that might warn adults about being overly curious or seeking novelty when considerable risk is involved is also low in teenagers. As a consequence, teenagers frequently seek novel experiences or may try to satisfy their curiosity about unfamiliar or intriguing situations without considering the possibility of risk or the serious ramifications of such behaviors.

4. A - use-it-or-lose-it process

Brain growth and development in teenagers is essentially a use-it-or-lose-it process. The brain's ability to acquire and retain new information as well as the reliability and the degree of connectivity of the brain's neural pathways are largely influenced by the quality, type, and number of experiences that teenagers receive. For example, learning to play a musical instrument while reading sheet music appears to require the activation of as many as eight different areas of the teenage brain (Fick & Shilts, 2006). Scientists now know that the brain has the ability to change its organization and structure—an aspect known as plasticity—as the result of sensory stimulation. Neural connections that get used and exercised are strengthened and retained while those that are not get pruned away. Dr. Richard Haier, of the University of California at Irvine College of Medicine, reports that general human intelligence appears to be based upon the volume of gray matter in certain areas of the brain and that it is likely that a person's mental abilities depends largely on the individual pattern of gray matter across his or her brain (cited in University of California, Irvine, 2004). For example, learning other languages during the early adolescent years often creates gray matter in those areas of the brain that process language information in much the same way as exercise builds muscles. Jay Giedd asserts that "teens have the power to determine (the direction of) their own brain development, to determine which connections survive and which don't. Whether they do art, or music or sports, or video games," it is those brain structures that are adapted accordingly (cited in Begley, 2000, p. 58).

Figure 3.2 Use It or Lose It: Teenagers Have the Power to Determine the Development of Their Own Brains

Music and Performing Arts

Academic Research and investigation

Drama, Role Playing, and Simulations

Social Interaction and Collaboration

Athletics and Physical Movement

Visual Arts

Brain Games and Other Challenges

"Teens have the power to determine their own brain development."

Jay Giedd, cited in "Getting Inside a Teen Brain" by Sharon Begley, 2000, p. 58

5. Overreliance on the amygdala:

Teenagers appear to process emotions differently from adults, using the amygdala (the emotional center of the brain) more than the frontal lobe (particularly in early adolescence). This gradually shifts as the teen grows older. Overreliance on the amygdala may explain why adolescents so frequently misread emotional signals. Recent studies by Robert McGiven and his colleagues (cited in "Teen Angst Rooted in Brain," 2002) found that as children reach puberty, their ability to quickly recognize and read social situations and emotions in others dropped by as much as 20% and gradually returned to normal abilities by age 18.

6. Shifts in the activation areas in the brain for certain skills:

During the teen years, there appears to be shifts in the activation areas of the brain for certain skills (e.g., language skills). The areas of activity may move from other lobes of the brain to the frontal lobes, or additional areas of the brain may become active to aid in the processing of this sensory information. Language capacity appears to be primarily restricted to one hemisphere of the brain prior to adolescence (i.e., chiefly in the left hemisphere for right-handed persons and vice versa), but by age 20–25, the capacity for language skills appears to become more evenly distributed between the hemispheres (cited in American Academy of Neurology, 2004). In addition, improved neural connections during the teen years in two areas of the brain called Wernicke's area and Broca's area are thought to be linked to improved language comprehension, speech, and writing proficiency in adolescents.

7. Greater need for proper nutrition, rest, and sleep:

Because of rapid physical growth spurts and brain development changes, adolescents generally have greater nutritional needs and require increased amounts of quality rest and sleep. Rest is crucial to the brain's ability to remember things and to function at optimal levels in learning tasks.

8. Physical growth spurts and changes in the cerebellum:

Significant changes and development in the cerebellum coupled with physical growth spurts likely explain the periods of clumsiness and awkwardness that most teenagers experience. As the cerebellum develops and matures, motor skills and body coordination improve. Since it is believed that the cerebellum also has a significant role in the coordination of a number of higher-level thought processes, physical activity and varied movement experiences can be particularly helpful to the developing teenage brain.

9. More abundant and active sex hormones:

During adolescence sex hormones are especially abundant and active in the brain, particularly the brain's emotional center. These chemicals directly influence the neurochemicals that affect and regulate mood and excitability, perhaps explaining why teenagers are more prone to rapid mood changes and frequently demonstrate an appetite for strong sensations, impulsivity, excitement, and risk taking.

10. Greater susceptibility to addictions:

Rapid changes are also noted in the levels of certain other neurotransmitter chemicals such as serotonin and dopamine, which control and regulate the pleasure response in the brain. Alcohol, nicotine, and many other such drugs appear to trigger much of the same response in the brain as these natural neurotransmitters. Consequently, using such drugs during a time period when there are frequent and significant fluctuations in the levels of these neurotransmitter chemicals appears to make teenagers more susceptible and vulnerable to addictions of all types. Addictions that begin in the adolescent years are also significantly more difficult to overcome.

11. Permanent and damaging results from the use and abuse of toxins and drugs:

The critical developmental changes occurring in the teenage brain and the general plasticity of the adolescent brain make it more susceptible to permanent changes and damaging results from the use and abuse of many different toxins and chemicals. Hard-core drugs like cocaine, heroin, and speed can cause permanent changes in the brain. In particular, the drug ecstasy may cause severe damage to brain cells in the teenage brain. Although for many years, scientists believed that alcohol and nicotine had relatively fewer damaging effects (at least no more than with adults) in the teenage brain, research now is beginning to show otherwise. Studies cited by Barbara Strauch (2003) in *The Primal Teen: What the New Discoveries About the Teenage Brain Tell Us About Our Kids* suggest that alcohol and nicotine cause permanent changes and probable damage in adolescent brains. Scott Swartzwelder, of Duke University, states, "We know the teenage brain is different, and one way that it's different is that it seems to be more sensitive to alcohol" (cited in Strauch, 2003, p. 179). Many researchers are saying that in light of what we now know about the developing teenage brain we need to raise the red flag about substance use (including nicotine and alcohol) and its long-term effects (likely permanent) on the adolescent brain.

12. First appearances of most psychiatric and mental disorders:

Most psychiatric and mental disorders (e.g., schizophrenia, bipolar disorder, severe depression) first appear in the adolescent years. This may suggest that many of these can be linked to problems with myelination, pruning of gray matter, and/or the over- or underproduction of such brain chemicals as dopamine. It may be that these processes expose or exacerbate dysfunctional areas or uncover poorly operating neural networks in the brain. In addition to these serious disorders, teens generally appear to be more susceptible to the effects of long-term stress (Strauch, 2003).

LOOKING BACK AT PART I— REFLECTION AND REVIEW

Targeting the Key Points!

- What we know about the teenage brain and how it is developing has changed dramatically over the past few years.
- Adolescence is a time when dynamic and significant changes occur in the teenage brain.
- There are a number of different stages and phases in adolescence.
- Much of the behavior of teenagers can be explained by biological changes taking place in the brain.
- The development of the teenage brain is often a case of use it or lose it.
- The development of the teenage brain depends largely upon the kinds and quality of experiences it receives. Teenagers have the opportunity to determine the future development of their brains through the activities and experiences in which they choose to engage.
- Teenagers process emotions differently than adults.
- Teenagers do more of their thinking and decision making in the emotional parts of their brains.
- The last part of the teenage brain to fully mature is that part in which higher-level thinking and more rational decision making occurs.

Some Questions to Ponder

What is the most significant thing I have learned about the teenage brain?

What does this new information about the teenage brain mean for me?

In what ways should my assumptions and perceptions about teenagers be changed?

In what ways will this new understanding of teenagers affect the way I work with and interact with teenagers?

Ten Powerful Ideas for Unleashing the Potential of the Teenage Brain

10
Time and Timing

1
Constructing
New Knowledge

9
Social Interaction
and Learning

2
Different Ways
of Learning

8
Reflection and
Self-Assessment

3
Making Meaning,
Connections,
and Patterns

7
Memory, Learning,
and Emotion

4
Whole-Brain
Learning

6
Physical Activity
and Movement

5
Multiple Memory
Pathways

PART II

Ten Powerful Ideas About the Brain and Learning and What It Means for Teaching the Teenage Brain

What have we learned from neuroscience, cognitive research, and educational theory about teaching teenagers? What can we take from the ideas and theories of earlier and current researchers, educators, and writers who have examined how we learn, who have expanded upon the concept of intelligence, or who have described the application of neuroscience to pedagogy? Can we distill from this worksome fundamental truths or ideas that, where applied appropriately in the classroom, will result in significantly more effective teaching and learning? The answer is a resounding YES! Part II (Chapters 4–13) of this text describes 10 fundamental, powerful ideas that encapsulate or summarize much of the work of these other researchers and educators into a conceptual framework that will help teachers to make their teaching brain compatible and their classrooms much more engaging for those unpredictable teenage brains!

4

Powerful Idea #1

Constructing New Knowledge

Teenagers learn by actively constructing new knowledge based upon their prior experiences and understandings. This powerful idea describes the most commonly held current theory about knowledge and learning. This theory, based initially on the work of Piaget (1952) and Vygotsky (1978) and extensively elaborated upon later by Jerome Bruner (1966), is known as *constructivism*. Bransford, Brown, and Cocking (2000), in the text *How People Learn: Brain, Mind, Experience, and School*, write, "The contemporary view of learning is that people construct new knowledge and understanding based on what they already know and believe" (p. 10). Constructivism is a way of explaining how people come to know and understand the world around them. Learning is chiefly the result of the brain constructing new mental models as it fits and connects new information to beliefs, concepts, and ideas already held. Thus the older learning becomes the foundation on which newer learning is constructed.

Reduced to the most basic form, learning is constructing meaning; without the construction of meaning, there is no learning. The construction of meaning is a mental process; thus to ensure that learners learn, experiences and activities must be provided to engage and activate the learner's mind. This construction of meaning is affected by the prior experiences of the learner, his or her beliefs and values, as well as the contexts in which the new learning occurs (i.e., how the prior knowledge is activated and the new learning reinforced and connected to the old).

Constructivism really implies that learning is a very personal experience and that all learners must be presented with experiences that will enable them to connect already existing concepts or knowledge bases to new ones.

> Learning is constructing meaning; without the construction of meaning, there is no learning.
>
> To ensure that learners learn, experiences and activities must be provided to engage and activate the learner's mind.

Therefore, the role of the teacher is to create experiences and learning opportunities where the teacher can observe what the student previously believed and help the student personally reconstruct new concepts or ideas that are valid and yet have unique individual meaning for the student.

Bruner (1966) stated that there are three important principles for constructivist teaching:

- Teaching must be focused on or concerned with the kinds of experiences and the contexts for learning that make the student willing and able to learn. In other words, the learner must be ready for and capable of the learning as presented.

- Teaching must be organized in such ways that it is easily grasped and understood by the learner. This calls for the spiral organization and scaffolding of new knowledge upon the previous.

- Finally, teaching needs to be designed in ways that will allow the learner to extrapolate or apply the new knowledge to new situations or fill in gaps of understanding.

Various other writers (Brooks & Brooks, 1993; Ernest, 1995; Jonassen, 1991; von Glasersfeld, 1995) have discussed the characteristics of classrooms and teaching (Figure 4.1) that are based upon a constructivist model.

Figure 4.1   Some Characteristics of Constructivist Classrooms

- Teacher serves as guide, mentor, coach, and facilitator.
- Learning tasks are presented in real-world contexts.
- Primary materials and other authentic data are often used.
- Construction of new knowledge is emphasized rather than reproduction of teacher's knowledge.
- Problem-based learning and higher-order thinking skills are emphasized.
- Emphasis is on conceptual interrelatedness and interdisciplinary learning.
- Students are exposed to multiperspectives and alternative viewpoints.
- Collaborative and cooperative learning is stressed.
- Authentic assessment is used, giving frequent feedback about learning.

WHAT POWERFUL IDEA #1 MEANS FOR TEACHERS: HELPING TEENAGERS CONSTRUCT PERSONAL MEANING

Learning is an active process in which students must be individually engaged. Teachers need to provide and orchestrate learning activities and experiences where students can activate their own prior knowledge and then use this prior knowledge to reconstruct new meaning. It implies that learning needs to be both active and personal where students have ample opportunities to call up and examine their own understandings and beliefs about various concepts and ideas in light of new information. Students need to be able to review older ideas and beliefs, test out and apply new knowledge, and reconstruct new models based upon their personal understandings. Teachers need to recognize that all learners will bring their own unique ideas, interpretations, and understandings about any idea or concept. Because of the evolving nature of the teenage brain, the teacher's role in providing a constructivist learning environment is both daunting and crucial for these learners. Care must be taken to ensure that the adolescent learner is ready and receptive for the teaching experience. For example, adolescents, particularly younger ones, often will need short, concrete experiences as opposed to more abstract ones with long-range payoffs because their brains are not ready to function at that higher cognitive level. Emotional teenagers quite frequently get frustrated when success is not immediate and need to be convinced that errors and mistakes are the way that the brain naturally learns and is normal. It is important to emphasize to teens that it takes time to learn; it does not happen instantaneously. Constructivist learning implies that learners constantly need to revisit ideas and concepts, think about them in other ways, and use them in other applications. It is common for teenagers to complain that they have been there or done that. Teenage learners need to be encouraged and guided in the examination of their own learning through carefully crafted self-reflection and self-assessment activities. Because we know that the areas of the brain that are used and exercised get reinforced and strengthened, adolescent learners need to experience a range of diverse methods, strategies, models, and approaches directed at examining complex concepts and real-world situations and problems. Learning needs to be particularly contextual for the teenage brain. Teenagers often require help and guidance in seeing the "grays" of the world rather than only the sharply demarcated black and white they might normally see. Instructional techniques such as problem-based learning or inquiry force teenagers to utilize more of the parts of the brain that deal with decision making, prioritizing, and organizing information. Such methods also help teenagers to see and appreciate the consequences of certain actions or decisions.

> Constructivist learning implies that learners constantly need to revisit ideas and concepts, think about them in other ways, and use them in other applications.

Often teachers will need to provide the short-term, more external motivation for certain learning tasks because the teenage mind might see not see or appreciate the more long-term rewards. Teachers need to develop strategies and techniques that will allow students to activate prior knowledge, but will also allow teachers to observe the beliefs, values, and ideas currently held by students. Teenagers need to come to understand and appreciate that everything we learn is in relationship to our own beliefs, values, and ideas about the world. This is a gradual process—one that undoubtedly requires the entire teenage years as students' brains develop the ability to think on this higher level. Sometimes the teacher will need to facilitate and guide students in their personal construction of knowledge when it is evident that their understandings are incomplete, incorrect, or based upon faulty assumptions or beliefs.

HOW IT MIGHT LOOK—A CASE STUDY

Saving the Old Victoria Street School

As you read the following case study, consider the following questions:

1. How was Ms. MacLeod able to use the concern of one of her students to create an authentic learning experience?

2. In what ways is Ms. MacLeod's role different from that of a more traditional social studies teacher?

3. What made this learning event so powerful for Ms. MacLeod's students?

4. Can you think of some situations where you might use this approach in your own teaching?

One Monday, one of Ms. MacLeod's students, Ashanti, came to class quite visibly upset. When prompted, Ashanti revealed to the class that her father told her over the weekend that the town was going to tear down the old Victoria Street Grammar School building—the elementary school where she and many of her classmates had attended class. Indeed, Ashanti had discovered that both her father and mother and even her grandmother had attended the same school. She lamented that something should not be destroyed just because it is old. Ms. MacLeod saw this as a wonderful opportunity to use the class's sudden interest in the old school as a way to introduce her class to a problem-based approach to learning. She thought that this would be an opportune time to have her class conduct some legitimate and relevant historical research as well as examine how local government makes decisions. She asked her class if they wanted to try to do something about this issue. The class agreed that they would like to take on this challenge. With Ms. MacLeod's help and with the aid of some graphic organizers she provided, they were able to discuss and define the problem more precisely, and brainstorm some ideas about what they might do. Ms. MacLeod guided the class into reflecting upon what they already knew about the problem, charting possible solutions, identifying what the class believed might be the best course of action, and finally considering what additional information they needed to have. She asked her students to think carefully about such questions as, "Who is the town?" "Why might the town want to tear the old school down?" "Would there be some value in preserving the old school?" "Could it be used for something else?" "Who might actually make the final decision on this issue?" and "How might we influence these decision makers?" They soon realized that they needed to collect some information about the school and to do some research about saving old buildings. Within a few days, several of the students discovered that some older buildings can be designated as historical sites. Ms. MacLeod asked her class to carefully consider what they now knew in terms of the possible solutions that they had identified earlier. By doing so, the class agreed that they needed to refocus their efforts. The class decided that they needed to find out which types of buildings become historical sites, how old they need to be, whom you need to convince, and what procedures you need to follow to save a building and have it designated as a historical site. With Ms. MacLeod's help, the class outlined what they needed to do to determine if Victoria Street School could be designated as a historical site and what procedures or steps they would need to do to have it so designated. While conducting the research, the class also undertook a letter-writing campaign to the local newspaper, organized a survey of local residents, met with some local politicians, and were even successful in having the issue raised through the local television newscast. After several weeks, it was announced that the decision to tear down the old school would be postponed until it could be debated at a council meeting in two months time. The class quickly sought and received permission to make a presentation at this meeting. Another class-brainstorming session helped the students identify the kinds of information and type of presentation that they would need to convince the town council to save the old school. This has now become the new focus of their work. Throughout the entire process, Ms. MacLeod provided frequent opportunities for her class to reflect upon what they had learned, getting them to document their changing viewpoints and the ways in which their research influenced their decision making. Both Ms. MacLeod and her class agreed that this was one of the best social studies learning experiences that they had ever had.

Figure 4.2   Constructivist Teaching—The Problem-Solving Approach

- Teacher begins with a question or problem and gets students hooked on the problem. Students should see issue or problem as personally relevant.
- Teacher helps students to identify the problem and to brainstorm possible solutions and a plan of action.
- Teacher helps students to identify important questions and credible sources of research and ways of gathering information.
- Students conduct research and gather information.
- Teacher helps students to reevaluate options and decide upon a new course of action based on research.
- Students carry out action plan.
- Teacher assists students with reflecting upon the learning and decision making processes and with evaluating their success. This may lead to further questions and courses of action.

CONSTRUCTIVIST TEACHING STRATEGIES

Problem-based learning is a wonderful way to promote constructivist teaching in the classroom and is particularly suited to making learning relevant, experiential, and rooted in real-world situations. Service learning, inductive teaching such as Bruner's concept attainment model (Bruner, Goodnow, & Austin, 1986), interdisciplinary units, and the workshop approach are other teaching approaches that will lend themselves to constructivist teaching. Figure 4.3 describes some strategies and approaches that will promote active learning in the constructivist classroom.

Want to learn more about problem-based learning? Try these books:

How to Use Problem-Based Learning in the Classroom, Robert Delisle, 1997, Association for Supervision and Curriculum Development, Alexandria, VA.

Problems as Possibilities, Linda Torp and Sara Sage, 1998, Association for Supervision and Curriculum Development, Alexandra, VA.

Figure 4.3   Some Strategies and Approaches That Will Make Your Classroom More Constructivist

Strategy or Approach	Purpose and Benefit	Examples and Description
Activators and Advance Organizers	Assist students (and teacher!) to identify what they already know and create focus or attention in brain to help motivate learners.	*Four Corners*—Teacher poses a question and provides four possible answers (one posted in each corner)—students select their answer by standing in one of four corners. *Word Splash*—A page of randomly spaced words or terms about new topic shown on screen or as a handout page. *Class Continuum*—Teacher provides a continuum line from Really Know to Know Very Little about new topic, and students indicate where along the continuum they fall. *Picture This*—Teacher uses an unusual, controversial, or provocative image to get students thinking about or interested in new topic.
Student Start-Ups	Provide students with ownership and immediately get students involved in new topic or unit.	Group of three or four students is responsible for researching and providing introduction and context for next topic or unit of study.
Graphic Organizers (e.g., Concept Maps, Ideas Maps, or Mind Maps)	Help students summarize, organize, and reflect upon new and old learning.	Students are asked to develop an idea map called "Forces That Wear Down the Earth" at the beginning, middle, and end of earth sciences unit.
Case Studies and Role Playing	Give students more authentic real-world feel and application.	In biology class, students play the role of "disease detectives" by attempting to determine the source and spread of a contagion from historical data and trying to formulate theories about its spread.
Service Learning	Connects in-school learning with specific application to projects in community. Builds a sense of community and civic responsibility and stewardship.	Mr. V's biology class has been keeping statistics on fish species in a small river in their community prior to and after doing a stream restoration project.
Essential Questions (Wiggins & McTighe, 1998, p. 26-33)	Help students identify and focus on the most important aspect of the topic or subject; provide relevance and show interrelationships; help students develop greater meaning.	Wiggins and McTighe describe questions as the "doorways to understanding" and "essential questions" as those that go to the heart of or key aspect of a subject and raise other important issues and questions. Using essential questions as the main organizing frame for a subject or topic will provide "sharper focus and a better direction for inquiry" for both teacher and students and will enable students to create greater meaning.

(Continued)

Figure 4.3 (Continued)

Workshop Approach	Students have the opportunity to practice and improve specific skills with coaching from the teacher through frequent conferencing and regular feedback.	A local history project, guided by the teacher who acts as coach and coresearcher, requires students to work on historical research and documentation skills.
Inductive Thinking and Teaching	Requires students to look for common characteristics or patterns in information or data to identify the common concept or idea. Designed to have students inductively build understanding of a concept or idea.	*Bruner's Concept Attainment Model*—Teacher provides various examples and nonexamples of a particular concept. Students attempt to identify common features and rules for the concept and extend their understanding by adding new examples and applying the concept in some way (Bruner, 1966). *Taba's Concept Formation Strategy*—Similar to Bruner's strategy, but students collect the data about a particular concept, analyze and group them, generalize the rules for the concept, and attempt to further apply data to show their understanding of concept (Taba, 1967).
Authentic Assessment	Helps students to identify end targets for learning and provides meaningful feedback to students as they strive to meet targets.	*Learning Logs*—Students establish learning goals and document their progress toward these goals. *Reflection Journals*—Using various prompts, students reflect upon what and how they have learned. *Personal Growth Portfolios*—A self-selected collection of student work to document their growth in understanding and learning during the unit of study.

Note: These strategies and approaches can also be found in the glossary.

5

Powerful Idea #2

Different Ways of Learning

Teenagers have different ways of learning. This idea really embodies two concepts: first, the premise that human intelligence is multifaceted and can be exhibited in a number of different ways; and second, that teenagers, like all persons, have different styles or ways of learning.

> Every human brain is different and uniquely organized!

BEING SMART—HUMAN INTELLIGENCE

Over the past two decades, numerous writers and theorists on this subject have largely refuted the ideas on what constitutes human intelligence that were so prevalent for nearly the entire twentieth century. Previously, the commonly held view was that human intelligence was largely determined by genetics and that it could be easily measured and quantified by a numerical quotient. In this model, intelligence was restricted to a narrow range of abilities—largely mathematical and linguistic—and was considered to be unchangeable beyond birth. Beginning in the 1980s, a number of writers and researchers began to challenge this widely accepted concept of intelligence. One of the first, Reuven Feuerstein, wrote in 1980 that his work led him to believe that intelligence was not a fixed entity but was rather a function of past learning and experience.

Other writers like Art Costa (1995), Robert Sternberg (1985), David Perkins (1986), and Howard Gardner (1983) have supported and reinforced this view. Certainly no researcher has done more to expand the notion of what constitutes human intelligence than Howard Gardner, who in his 1983 book *Frames of Mind: The Theory of Multiple Intelligences* first developed the idea that intelligence was multifaceted and that humans exhibited various types of intelligences in many different ways. Daniel Goleman (1995) with his work on emotional intelligence and Costa (1995) who described and defined a set of intelligent behaviors or traits expanded this concept of intelligence as being multidimensional and a function of experience and learning. Today human intelligence is generally seen as being multifaceted and not easily quantifiable. Often, it is best exhibited during problem solving and measured in a more real-world context. Intelligence is also seen as developmental and changeable throughout one's lifetime. Since each brain is unique and it changes through learning, the concept of intelligence is now used to try and understand human intellectual capacity and the many and diverse ways people can learn and demonstrate their understanding. Current ideas about human intelligence are summarized in Figure 5.1.

Figure 5.1   What We Believe About Human Intelligence!

- Every brain is uniquely organized.
- Intelligence is multidimensional and multifaceted.
- Intelligence is not easily quantifiable and measurable.
- Intelligence can be exhibited in many ways.
- Intelligence is developmental and changeable throughout one's lifetime.
- The best way to gauge intelligence is often by observing how it is exhibited during problem solving in real-world situations.

PREFERRED WAYS OF LEARNING— OUR LEARNING STYLES

Perhaps the first major efforts in educational literature and research aimed at convincing teachers that they need to see their students as different learners came through the literature on learning styles. It has now become widely accepted in educational circles that people exhibit and prefer to use different learning styles and modalities. Since the 1970s, a number of educational and psychological researchers have developed models to describe various learning styles or modalities. Among these are Katherine Briggs and Isabel Myers (1977), Bernice McCarthy (1980), Anthony Gregorc (1979), Rita and Kenneth Dunn (1993), and J. R. Hanson and Harvey Silver (1998). There are a number of others, including the currently popular learning and personality styles inventory called True Colors developed in 1984 by Educational Consultant Sandi Redenback. These writers attempt to describe the various styles of learners by focusing on the learning process and how the learner goes through this process as well as by examining the learner's personality and how he or she perceives, interacts with, and responds to the learning experience.

Learning styles really describe how learners go about learning—how individuals learn best!

Learning styles can be thought of as different and distinctive cognitive, emotional, personality, and physiological behaviors or traits that are unique to a particular individual and can predict how that individual will respond in a learning situation. Thus, learning styles can be simply thought of as the learner's preferred way of using his or her abilities to learn. It really describes how learners go about learning. It is important to recognize that learning styles are neither good nor bad. They just are. Every student's style of learning needs to be validated, valued, and appreciated. Learning styles tend to evolve and change as a person grows older, so it should not be thought of as a fixed characteristic that is immutable. In addition, learners might exhibit different learning styles in different situations; for example, a student might behave (i.e., learn) in different ways in an English class as opposed to studying for a driver's test or learning the playbook for the basketball team.

Learning styles are neither GOOD nor BAD. They just are!

It is very important to remember that every teacher will also have his or her own preferred learning style and most frequently will end up teaching in that style. Regrettably, this can cause significant problems in the classroom. Mike Hughes (1999), in *Closing the Learning Gap*, concludes that it is safe to assume that as many as two thirds of the students sitting in a typical classroom will have a different learning modality from the teacher. Although some students can adapt and learn outside their preferred learning styles, others find it very difficult to do so. It seems that, in particular, the group of students that prefer a kinesthetic style of learning finds it difficult to adapt to other modalities of learning. Clearly it is important for teachers to become knowledgeable about their own learning styles as well as those of their students in order to facilitate effective learning for all students in their classrooms. Barrie Bennett and Carol Rolheiser (2001), authors of *Beyond Monet—The Artful Science of Instructional Integration*, feel that providing information about learning styles encourages teachers to have a more extensive understanding of how students learn and will lead teachers to develop a greater repertoire of ways to involve students in their learning. They argue that learning about learning styles increases a teacher's "conceptual flexibility" about how to respond to the diverse ways in which students learn (Bennett & Rolheiser, 2001).

WHAT POWERFUL IDEA #2 MEANS FOR TEACHERS: TEACHING TO EACH UNIQUE BRAIN

It is difficult to not overemphasize the significance and importance of this powerful idea in assisting teachers to unleash the potential of the teenage brain. Neuroscientists have little doubt that the growth and development of the brain depends a great deal on the quantity, kinds, and types of experiences that the brain has. Cognitive researchers clearly feel that intelligence is developmental and changeable throughout one's lifetime. The adolescent years may be a particularly critical period in the development of the brain and intelligence. Neuroscientists Harry Chugani and Charles Nelson have little doubt that experiences "alter the developing synapse-rich brains of adolescents" (cited in Strauch, 2003, p. 42). Jay Giedd suggests that adolescence is "a stage of development when the environment or activities of the teenager may guide" and determine the nature of brain development and growth during adolescence (cited in Strauch, 2003, p. 44).

> The teenage years are a use-it-or-lose-it time for brain development!

Many researchers have described this critical period in the development of the brain (i.e., the teen years) as a use-it-or-lose-it time. Those areas (and the respective neurons and synapses) in the brain that get used and reinforced through experiences become strengthened and more efficient and are less likely to be pruned and pared away. Jay Giedd (Fanning 2002), in an interview on the PBS program *Inside the Teenage Brain*, quite dramatically stated the case when he said, "So if a teen is doing music or sports or academics, those are the cells and connections that will be hardwired. If they're lying on the couch or playing video games or MTV, those are the cells and connections that are going to survive" (Fanning, 2002). The brain becomes smarter by adding new knowledge to the old and by activating existing neural networks. This means that the more varied and diverse learning experiences we can provide to the evolving teenage brain, the more intelligent and capable it becomes—able to utilize many different ways of processing information through a number of different facets and dimensions of intelligence.

> The brain becomes smarter by adding new knowledge to the old and by activating existing neural networks.

Teachers really need to understand that every teenage brain that they encounter in their teaching is different and unique—different in the abilities and intelligences it possesses and different in the ways that it learns. Not only is it unique, but also it has the potential to become smarter and more proficient as it processes many different types of learning experiences and sensory input. Consequently, teachers need to provide diverse and varied learning experiences for students so that the curriculum and learning can be accessed by all students through their own emerging and unique intelligences and learning styles.

> It is vitally important for teachers to utilize instructional strategies and experiences that will challenge all types of intelligence, promote growth in different facets of intelligence, and acknowledge every student's unique patterns of intelligence.

The literature on learning styles and modalities provides an additional window into how students learn. Teachers need to become knowledgeable about learning styles and different modalities of learning by accessing this literature. With this knowledge base, teachers should begin to understand and appreciate that their students learn in many different ways and that their role in facilitating effective learning for all their students is a very challenging and sometimes daunting task. However, there are steps that teachers can take after acquiring this additional insight. First, through observation and by using a variety of the learning styles inventories, teachers need to try and describe or classify the learning styles of their students and then share this information with their students. Examining learning styles with your students and having them determine their own personal styles is a very valuable learning experience. One of the most empowering ways in which teachers can assist their students is to help them understand how they learn and in what ways. Equipped with the knowledge of who they are as learners and through the validation of their own unique strengths and abilities, students can become convincing advocates for their own learning needs. Students will also develop a healthy respect and empathy for the other students around them. Teachers need, as well, to carefully examine their own learning and teaching styles to ensure that their styles do not become the predominant mode utilized in the classroom. Finally, and most important, teachers need to ensure that they use a varied and diverse range of instructional strategies and processes in their classes so that all students have ample opportunities to learn in their preferred styles. Figure 5.2 provides some ideas to assist teachers in helping their students understand their brains and their learning styles.

Figure 5.2   Some Things Teachers Can Do to Help Their Students Understand
Their Brains and How They Learn

- Become knowledgeable about multiple intelligences and learning styles.
- Teach your students about their brains and how they change during learning.
- Teach students about multiple intelligences and learning styles.
- Provide inventories and assessment techniques to help students determine their intelligences and learning styles.
- Provide opportunities for all students to learn at times in their preferred ways.
- Challenge students and provide opportunities to learn in ways other than their preferred ways.
- Celebrate the range and diversity of intelligences and learning styles in your students.

UNLEASHING THE POTENTIAL OF THE TEENAGE BRAIN—SIX THINGS YOU OUGHT TO DO

1. Teach students about multiple intelligences and learning styles. Assist them to assess and identify their own particular strengths, abilities, and learning styles and the ways these impact their learning. Use common names and distinctive symbols to help students remember and associate their multiple intelligences and learning styles profiles with specific tasks and ways of learning. For example, music smart, body smart, or word smart for various intelligences or perhaps a magnifying glass to represent visual learning activities.

2. Consciously and deliberately develop and match instructional strategies and learning experiences to all the types of student intelligences and learning styles in your classroom.

3. Provide activities and grouping structures in your classrooms where students are required to work cooperatively and utilize the complementary intelligences and learning styles of other students to complete the learning task.

4. Have your students compile multiple intelligences and learning styles portfolios where they must include learning tasks and activities that demonstrate a variety of intelligences and ways of learning.

5. Diversify and differentiate the activities for a particular unit or topic of study by using multiple intelligences and learning styles learning centers or task cards.

6. Address multiple intelligences and learning styles in your classroom with contract learning. The requirements for the learning contract can be set up so that students must work in a variety of student groupings (individual, pairs, or small group) and need to complete activities or assignments that draw upon a variety of intelligences and utilize different learning styles.

HOW IT MIGHT LOOK—A CASE STUDY

Ms. Taylor's Meteorology Unit

As you read the following case study, consider the following questions:

1. How has Powerful Idea #2 influenced Ms. Taylor's instructional planning?

2. In what ways is Ms. Taylor challenging all types of intelligences and promoting growth in different facets of intelligence?

3. What would Ms. Taylor need to know about her students before using this instructional approach in her class?

4. What benefits can you see to using learning centers to facilitate teaching and learning?

The students in Ms. Taylor's integrated science class are studying a unit in meteorology. Her students work in learning groups of four students. Ms. Taylor has organized the groups for this learning experience because she wants the groups to have a diversity of abilities, intelligences, and learning preferences. She explains this carefully to her students who all understand that, at other times, they will get to work in self-selected groups. For the four-week unit, Ms. Taylor has set up a series of learning activity centers. There are sufficient centers set up so that there are more centers than groups and thus some centers are always open. At the front of the class, there is a directory board that lists all the centers with a color-coded directory card to match with each center. As all of the groups decide upon a particular center, they remove a card from the directory indicating that the center is being used. The card is then returned to the main directory when the group is finished with that center.

Each center is arranged so that there are four different tasks at each center. These tasks focus on different aspects of the curricular content and utilize different intelligences, abilities, and learning styles. At each center, each group must divide the tasks so that each member is working on a different one. When all students have finished their separate tasks, there is a summary activity that requires each student to teach the other group members and then collectively compile the information and data from the four separate tasks. When all the work at all centers has been finalized, each group is required to complete a concluding review and summary assignment and turn in a log book detailing all the centers and the activities completed at each. At the beginning of the unit, Ms. Taylor works with her students to develop a grading rubric that is used to evaluate the work completed during this unit. The rubric includes opportunities for both the teacher and group members to evaluate and reflect upon their work.

Powerful Idea #3

Making Meaning, Connections, and Patterns

The teenage brain always seeks meaning and needs to make connections and develop patterns. The human brain has a wonderful capacity to take in a huge quantity of seemingly disconnected and isolated information and integrate it with or connect it to what is already known. However, it appears that the brain takes in and organizes sensory information in a random fashion rather than in any sequential and logical way. Instead, it appears to look for patterns to which it can attach new information. The brain is constantly seeking meaning—it does so by looking for these patterns, associations, and linkages between what it already knows and any new information it receives. In fact, it seems that the brain not only seeks patterns, but also actually predicts or anticipates certain patterns based upon what it has previously learned. It is apparent that as soon as sensory information enters the brain, the brain and all its neural networks immediately determines if this new information is something it knows and/or could be connected to something it knows. These connections or patterns provide the context for any new information. If this context is absent, then the new information is likely to be discarded as irrelevant and meaningless.

Pattern making is the key to the teenage brain learning!

Pattern making appears to assist the brain in generating new memories (i.e., creating new learning) by linking or connecting prior learning with the new learning. Jane Healy (1994) describes this patterning process as "organizing and associating new information with previously developed mental hooks" (Healy, 1994, p. 49). Caine and Caine (1994) write, "The brain is designed to perceive and generate patterns, and it resists having meaningless patterns imposed on it. 'Meaningless' patterns are isolated pieces of information unrelated to what makes sense to a student" (p. 89).

As an expert in child development, Healy (1994) believes that pattern making may be an innate feature of our developing brain and a key to intelligence. It is something that babies and very young children do instinctively. For example, nearly all children learn to speak their mother's language despite the fact that it is perhaps the most difficult task that the brain ever accomplishes. Children do this by listening to the constant cacophony of sounds and language around them, sorting out the patterns and eventually assimilating these into language of their own. Children who grow up in language-deprived environments usually have significant language and learning problems for the remainder of their lives because their brains were unable to form the crucial language patterns in their brains at a vital time in their brain development. It appears to be critical to a child's mental growth that the pattern-detecting-and-making areas of the brain are developed. Children who are taught to look for patterns and connections early in life and through their elementary schooling do better in later grades when they must deal with information on the higher levels of comprehension such as the application, analysis, or synthesis of new information. It is clear that students at all levels should have ample opportunities to seek and to form patterns and connections during their learning experiences. Caine and Caine (1994) conclude that "the ideal process is to present the information in a way that allows brains to extract patterns, rather than attempt to impose them" (p. 90).

It seems likely that adolescence may very well be another of those critical times for the brain to further develop, refine, and consolidate its pattern-making capacity. It appears that as numerous neural pathways either are being newly established, strengthened, or pruned away in many different areas of the brain, the teenage brain becomes increasingly better at detecting and unraveling more sophisticated and complex patterns, connections, and relationships. Many parents and teachers will recognize the phenomena of the "aha moment" when teenagers suddenly seem to make sense out of something that they had been struggling with for some time. The puzzle pieces just seem to fall together for them. Undoubtedly this is due to their brains now being able to detect the patterns and make the requisite connections that are necessary for more complete understanding. At other times, this greater understanding comes more gradually and in stages as the teenage brain develops sufficiently and receives the kinds of learning experiences it needs to develop the required neural connections that enable it to perceive and make sense of the patterns and relationships. One often sees this evolution in teenagers in such diverse areas as language development, interpersonal and communication skills, mathematical reasoning, and the shift from concrete to more abstract thinking.

WHAT POWERFUL IDEA #3 MEANS FOR TEACHERS: DEVELOPING PATTERN MAKING AND DETECTING ABILITIES

The implications of this probable development in the pattern-making abilities of the teenage brain are two-fold. One implication is that for some types of learning and understanding, the aspect of readiness, which we often apply to younger children, also applies to teenagers. For example, to move to the higher-level abstract symbolic understanding required in more advanced mathematics, the teenage brain must be wired in ways that the brain will be able to perceive and make sense of the necessary patterns and relationships—that is, it must ready to make the shift to higher-order thinking. Second, it makes sense that effective teaching at this age level would utilize and include ample and diverse examples of increasingly complex patterns, connections, and relationships to assist the teenage brain in establishing the necessary neural networks needed to make it an effective pattern-making and -detecting organism.

The construction of meaning and true understanding is very individual and personal and comes about only when the brain is able to detect and make patterns and see connections and relationships. Students need lots of opportunities to do this. Teachers need to organize their teaching and their instructional approaches in such ways that their students are able to construct their own personal meaning and enhance their pattern-making and -detecting abilities.

Figure 6.1   Ten Questions You Can Ask to Enhance Pattern-Making Abilities

---

1. How is ___ like ___?

2. How is this different from or the same as?

3. What do you think or predict will happen next?

4. What patterns can you see in this?

5. How do these fit together?

6. What would happen if?

7. Can you create a rule for this?

8. Are these in the correct order? Can you put these in the correct order?

9. How is this related to? Are these all examples of?

10. What will follow this?

SOME STRATEGIES FOR YOU TO CONSIDER

Since the brain is such a natural pattern-making organ, certain pedagogical approaches would appear to be a good fit. Jensen (1998c), in *Teaching With The Brain In Mind*, suggests that using such instructional models as integrated thematic, interdisciplinary, or cross-disciplinary instruction makes good sense because in such models both teachers and students are challenged to see the themes, connections, and relationships of the wider fields of study. This can create deeper understanding and greater relevance for students as they explore and come to recognize the myriad links and relationships that exist among what are often treated as seemingly unrelated and disconnected areas of study. Here are some other ideas you might use:

- Use lots of patterning techniques and devices like graphic organizers, charts, graphs, sequence charts, flow diagrams, timelines, concept maps, or mind maps in the classroom.

- Use numerous hands-on, experiential learning experiences that connect to real-world situations.

- Utilize analogies, metaphors, and similes as ways for students to demonstrate their knowledge and understanding; for example, you might ask how photosynthesis is like a factory, like baking a cake, or some other reaction.

- Introduce students to and familiarize them with numerous examples of patterns and comparisons.

- Use questioning techniques (see Figure 6.1) that require students to compare, contrast, sort out, predict, or look for relationships, associations, and connections.

- Use the visual and performing arts to demonstrate and illustrate patterns. For example, have students draw a large diagram on the classroom floor or dance through the water cycle.

- Help students look for and identify patterns in the natural world; for example, insect cycles, bird calls, plant cycles, ecosystems.

- Ensure that students use numerous manipulatives and other concrete materials to form patterns and illustrate concepts in the classroom. For example, using Alge-tile* and other mathematics manipulatives to solve equations and illustrate mathematical concepts.

Note: Alge-tiles are commercially produced colored tiles that are used to teach and assist students with algebra and other abstract mathematical concepts.

HOW IT MIGHT LOOK—A CASE STUDY

Mrs. Parasiuk's Poetry Class

As you read this case study, look for,

- The ways that the teacher is developing the pattern-making and pattern-detection abilities of her students.

- Some ways that the teacher might use to evaluate how successful her students are at pattern detection.

Mrs. Parasiuk's Grade 8 students are examining rhyming schemes and patterns. She first conducts a short whole-class minilecture on what is meant by rhyming schemes and how to decode and summarize them. She provides several examples for the whole class, ensuring that through class discussion everyone understands the concept. Mrs. Parasiuk is using the jigsaw group method for this activity and uses the four lines from a short poem to assign her students to their home base groups. (Note: The jigsaw method is explained fully in Powerful Idea #9 as well as in the glossary of strategies.) Each student receives a piece of paper with one line of poetry on it, and the working groups are formed when four students combine their four pieces of paper to form a complete poem. In each home base group, learning partners take a simple poem, decode its rhyming pattern, and share with the whole group. The home groups then break into expert groups where each expert group receives a package containing several poems that are all typical of a particular rhyming scheme. The expert groups decode the rhyming schemes to detect the common pattern and use a reference list of rhyming schemes and patterns to determine the literary name for this pattern. As the expert groups are working, Mrs. Parasiuk moves from group to group asking a few questions (e.g., "What did you look for in this rhyming scheme?" "What is the pattern in this poem?" "How did you know that this poem fits that scheme?" "Are any of these poems alike in their rhyming schemes?") that clearly indicate to her that the students are able to detect and classify the patterns. When the students return to their home groups, each home group must use a graphic organizer provided by the teacher to concisely summarize all the rhyming schemes from the expert groups by illustrating their patterns and literary names. All home groups are then given a new, more complex piece of poetry and must use their summary organizer to decode and classify the rhyming schemes or patterns in the new piece of poetry. Mrs. Parasiuk uses a ChecBric (an assessment tool developed by Lewin & Shoemaker, 1998) to evaluate how successful all of the groups were in classifying the schemes and patterns in the more complex piece of poetry.

7

Powerful Idea #4

Whole-Brain Learning

LEFT, RIGHT, OR BOTH BRAINS?

The teenage brain learns best when both sides of the brain are actively engaged. The cerebral cortex (the thinking part) of the brain is divided into left and right sides, or hemispheres. It is known that each hemisphere operates differently and processes different types of information (see Figure 7.1). The left hemisphere is often referred to as the analytical and logical side of the brain. It effectively deals with information as fragments or parts and processes this information in a sequential fashion. Reading, writing, and listening are important processes that take place in the left hemisphere. The right hemisphere, known as the intuitive or creative side of the brain, prefers to process information randomly and as wholes. The right brain processes such sensory information as images, color, music, and spatial patterns. Although the two sides of the brain process information differently, it is now very clear that most learning involves both sides of the brain and that there is considerable connectivity between the two during any learning episode. Patricia Wolfe (2001) writes, "Although it now seems clear that our hemispheres each have their specialties, we must remember that they work in concert at all times" (p. 47).

A particularly important aspect to consider in the developing adolescent brain is the role of the corpus callosum in facilitating connectivity between the two hemispheres. We noted earlier in this text that, like many areas in the teenage brain, the corpus callosum is undergoing considerable thickening and

Figure 7.1 Left Brain or Right Brain?

Left Brain	Right Brain
Logical and analytical	Comfortable with randomness
Responds to verbal instructions	Responds to demonstrated instructions
Likes structure and organization	Likes open-endedness
Processes information as parts	Processes information as wholes
Looks at differences	Looks at similarities
Likes semantic information (words, facts, figures, data)	Likes images, color, pictures, spatial patterns
Prefers a sequential, ordered way of looking at things	Prefers fluidity, spontaneous, uncertain ways of looking at things
Often introverted, controlled emotions	Extroverted, more free with emotions
Is a splitter: wants to see cause and effect, predictability	Is a lumper: needs to see connectedness and resemblances

myelination during this time, greatly improving the communication between both sides of the brain. Since greater connectivity between the two hemispheres appears to improve creativity and problem-solving abilities, teaching teenagers in a more whole-brain way may be considerably more critical than we ever imagined.

> ## Secondary schools often overemphasize left-brain activities and experiences!

Secondary schools and many classrooms traditionally emphasize activities and experiences that are left-brain experiences—reading, writing, and listening are the dominant teaching and learning modes. The right hemisphere is often neglected. It is also quite widely accepted that every individual—this includes every student and of course, the teacher—tends to have a preferred hemisphere in which they frequently are more comfortable operating. Commonly teachers are highly verbal left-brain thinkers while many in their classes are more comfortable thinking and learning in their right brains. If the teacher persists in teaching in ways that are more consistent with their own hemispheric preference, many students will be disadvantaged. Teachers need to aware of this situation and attempt to provide a more balanced whole-brain approach. This can be accomplished by providing a wide variety of activities and experiences that ensure both sides of the brain are engaged and connected throughout the learning process.

WHAT POWERFUL IDEA # 4 MEANS FOR TEACHERS: EFFECTIVE WAYS TO MAKE YOUR CLASSROOM TEACHING WHOLE BRAIN

Teachers need to teach to both sides of the brain. Ideally, teachers should design diverse and rich learning experiences that will activate and engage both sides of the brain at the same time rather than constructing separate left- and right-brain activities. This can be done best by teaching new concepts and information as both parts and wholes and by embedding content within context; for example, one could teach mathematical concepts within the context of real-life applications. Whole-brain activities often combine visuals and graphic devices (drawing, pictures, diagrams, graphic organizers) with reading and writing activities. Using manipulatives and other concrete teaching materials as well as utilizing kinesthetic (i.e., movement and physical activity) approaches to teaching are other excellent ways to make teaching more whole brain. Figure 7.2 illustrates some strategies that teachers might incorporate into their teaching to make it more whole brain.

Some Other Ideas for You to Consider

- Consciously plan left-brain and right-brain options or approaches when introducing any new idea or concept.

- Alternate between teaching the big picture and the separate details (i.e., the trees and the forest).

- Provide experiences that assist students in seeing and appreciating a more global perspective (i.e., the big picture—how what they are learning fits into their lives or connects to the larger scheme of things).

- Present new concepts and information to students from quite different perspectives so that students are forced to see things differently and to use both sides of their brains.

- Provide direct instruction in skill development followed immediately by application and transfer to real life situations.

- Design assessments for both hemispheres of the brain, giving students options as to how they demonstrate their learning (e.g., performance assessments that combine skills and competencies from both sides of the brain).

- Ensure that right-brain activities (music, performing and visual arts, drama, role playing) are included in your repertoire of teaching strategies.

Figure 7.2   Eight Effective Ways to Make Your Classroom Teaching More Whole Brain

Strategy	How It Might be Used / Examples
Use both written and visual methods for note taking and summarizing	*Write It and Draw It* journal– a two-column journal where students write what they have learned in the left column and draw a pictorial or diagram in the right. *Four Corner Summary* – a graphic organizer divided into four squares. In one square students write the idea, term, or concept to be summarized; in another they draw a picture of the idea; in another they write how the idea is like or different from another idea; and in the final square, they draw a diagram to show a personal connection to the idea.
Sort Cards and/or Pictures	A series of terms or pictures related to topic being studied. Students must sort cards into related categories and then describe or write the reasons for their categories on a sorting table or chart.
Carousel Brainstorming	Teacher places several pieces of chart paper around classroom with a key question or idea on each one. Students circulate about room writing their individual ideas on each chart. Or, charts can be circulated around room from student to student. Students are encouraged to both write and sketch their ideas.
Mind Maps	Students use words, sketches, and/or symbols to map out their ideas, perceptions, or knowledge base about an idea or concept. Particularly powerful when students use colors.
Slow Reveal (Guillaume, Yopp, & Yopp, 2007)	A picture or image of a particular idea or concept is projected on a screen, but the image is covered up and slowly revealed bit by bit. Teachers can give a verbal clue each time as a piece is revealed. Students contribute their hypotheses after each reveal. After the image or concept is uncovered, students describe and explain which clues were most useful and how their thinking led them to identify the concept.
Quick Draws	When given a prompt, students must quickly draw what they understand about the idea or concept. For example, a teacher might ask students to draw something that would best represent our state, province, or county.
Placemat Brainstorming	Each group of students (works best with four) is given a large sheet of paper (e.g., 15" by 20") divided into four blocks with a central question or prompt written in the middle. At a signal from teacher, each student writes as much as he or she knows about the question in his or her block in one minute. Students then discuss the responses and decide upon which answers or responses best satisfy the question.
Word Journal (Angelo & Cross, 1993)	After a particular learning activity, unit, or topic, students are to review the information and select ONE word that best summarizes or encapsulates the topic and describe in their word journal in a couple of sentences why this word fits the topic so well. Students can use simple sketches or diagrams to aid as well.

Note: These strategies can also be found in the glossary.

HOW IT MIGHT LOOK—A CASE STUDY

Whole-Brain Assessment in Mr. Amos's Horticulture Class

As you read the following case study, consider the following questions:

1. What strategies or practices does Mr. Amos use to make his class more whole brain? In what ways could you use these strategies or practices in your classes?

2. In what ways is Mr. Amos' final assessment whole brain?

The students in Mr. Amos's introductory horticulture class participate in a wide variety of learning experiences throughout the year—laboratory sessions in the greenhouse, visits to commercial nurseries and landscaping businesses, online research about both native and nonnative plants, model and diorama making of various garden arrangements, mathematical calculations of plant nutrient requirements as well as reading and writing assignments on plant species, landscape design, and greenhouse management. Throughout the term, students have had opportunities to work individually, with learning partners, and in small groups. For the end-of-term assessment, the students are placed into design teams of three to four students and must research, plan, and design a horticultural and landscape plan for a particular property that the teacher assigns each design team. The final presentation must include both an oral summary and a visual display called a Z-chart. (A Z-chart is a presentation device designed by the author. It is two sheets of poster board—one cut into halves—hinged together with strong tape so that it can be freestanding in the shape of a large Z. Students have three or six different panels, front or both front and back, on which to display information.) Each panel of the Z-chart must be dedicated to one or more components of the information and research that Mr. Amos requires—a map and explanatory notes on the original property; design challenges, problems, and possibilities; suggested plants, ornamental shrubs, trees, and other design elements; two different landscape plans; and finally, a cost analysis. Mr. Amos provides time in class when his students work on their presentations and where he can provide coaching and guidance. He and his students collaboratively develop a grading rubric, as well, which will be used to evaluate the final product and presentation. Two weeks are set aside at the end of term during which time the teams must make their oral presentations. As they do so, they must refer frequently to their Z-chart displays. In addition, the entire class holds a horticulture exhibition night when community and family members are invited to the school auditorium where all the Z-charts are set up as displays, and students are present to answer questions about their projects. This project might also be done as a PowerPoint presentation or some other type of multimedia presentation.

8

Powerful Idea #5

Multiple Memory Pathways

The teenage brain learns most effectively when information and learning experiences can be placed into as many memory pathways as possible. Memory and learning are intricately connected. Keith Verner (2001) of the Pennsylvania State University College of Medicine has stated that "the way we perceive, attend to, process, and memorize information is at the heart of the issue of applying brain research to education" (p. 3). Although memory can be of two main types, short term and long term, learning is really about placing information into long-term memory so that it can be recalled or retrieved later. Long-term memory is not a thing, but rather a process. Long-term memories are not really stored in a particular place in the brain, but rather are the electrochemical connections or pathways, which were originally created when we first learned something, or the memory was first established. When we remember, these pathways or connections are recreated. It appears that we have a number of different types of memory pathways in our brain (and sometimes in other parts of our body) and that these different memory pathways can be established and retrieved in different ways—some easily, some with more difficulty.

DIFFERENT KINDS OF MEMORY— DECLARATIVE VERSUS PROCEDURAL

Various kinds of memory have been described in the research literature (see Figure 8.1). Many writers have described long-term memory in terms of being either declarative (explicit) memory, which deals with the what of information, and procedural (implicit) memory, which deals with the how of things.

Figure 8.1   Types of Memory Pathways

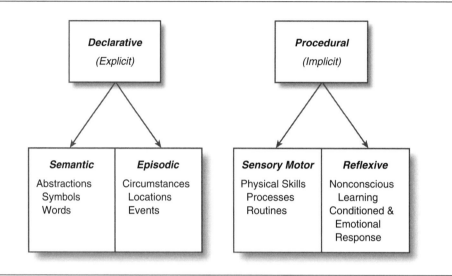

Declarative memory is often further subdivided into semantic and episodic memory while procedural memory can be subdivided into sensory motor and reflexive memories. Episodic memory refers to memories linked to specific events or circumstances in a person's life, for example, what you remember from your first date. This is often a strong memory pathway because it has such a strong emotional component to it. Semantic memory is described as the memory of meaning dealing with such abstract information as words, language, and isolated facts, figures, places, and things. Semantic memory is often quite difficult to establish and retrieve even when it is frequently and explicitly rehearsed or reviewed. Procedural memories relate to memories developed through motor skill connections, the recall of physical habits or routines, and, in the case of reflexive memories, automatic conditional responses, or emotional responses, for example, a person's reaction to touching a hot stove. Although these sometimes take more time to establish (think of learning to ride a bicycle), procedural memories are often very strong and can frequently be retrieved easily and without consciously trying to do so.

> There are at least four different ways of establishing memory pathways in the brain—semantic, episodic, procedural, and reflexive.

Although students do often need to learn semantic information, it needs to be embedded as much as possible in episodic and procedural memory. Most important, it appears that teaching that relies heavily on rote learning or learning unconnected information in isolation does not promote strong and persistent neural pathways since the brain does not like isolated information and needs to connect it with other things it knows. Recall or retrieval is better when teaching and learning occurs in a contextual, episodic, and experiential way or when memory is tied to sensory motor pathways—that is, through procedural memory.

> **Learning should be embedded as frequently as possible in episodic and procedural memory pathways.**

It is important to remind the reader again of the tremendous plasticity of the adolescent brain and dynamic growth happening in the teenage brain. As neural networks are consolidated and hardwired in the teenage brain, it is vitally important that this brain, with so much promise for learning, receives the full range of stimulation and experiences that will ensure that all memory pathways are activated and developed to the fullest potential. It speaks loudly and emphatically to us about the necessity of providing rich and varied learning experiences for the evolving teenage brain.

> **Learning is really about putting information into long-term memory!**

LEARNING AND MEMORY

Learning is really about putting information from many sensory sources into long-term memory. The brain is bombarded by innumerable bits of information every second. If it attended to every bit of information with equal importance, it could not cope. Thus it has mechanisms for handling all this information and deciding what to do with it. Most neuroscientists support the view that memory exists in different stages to allow the brain to decide how and what to do with all the sensory information it receives. A convenient model to use to describe how memory and learning work is the one proposed by Patricia Wolfe (2001) in *Brain Matters: Translating Research Into Classroom Practice.*

In this model, there are three stages of memory: sensory memory, short-term or working memory, and long-term memory. In Wolfe's model, all the information that the brain first receives ends up in sensory memory where it is held for fractions of a second until the brain decides what to do with it. Much of this information—as much as 99%—is almost immediately discarded because the brain judges it irrelevant or unimportant. Considerable information is dealt with unconsciously and reflexively while other information is directed to our conscious attention. If the brain judges that the information is important and requires our attention, it is shifted to short-term or working memory where we become consciously aware of it. Working memory is indeed very short term and transient. Estimates place it at about 15 to 20 seconds. This short duration allows our brain to temporarily store information until we can make further determination of what to do with it and yet still be able to discard it fairly quickly if we do not do something with it. Otherwise working memory would become overloaded and very inefficient.

However, to learn things (i.e., place it into long-term memory), we need to have some strategies to reinforce and retain this information longer and integrate it with already existing memories. Without these strategies to review or rework the information, it will not be transferred to the next stage—long-term memory—and thus will be lost. Reviewing, reworking, or practicing with the information will increase the time the information is held. Further application, elaboration, and reorganization will place it into long-term memory—thus, we have learned. Memory scientists call this process *rehearsal*.

> To learn things, we need to have strategies to reinforce and retain this information longer and integrate it with already existing memories.

Rehearsal Strategies

There are innumerable ways to rehearse information to retain it longer. Generally these rehearsal strategies are classified into two main categories: rote rehearsal and elaborative rehearsal. Rote rehearsal refers to that type of rehearsal procedure where one deliberately and continuously repeats the information, skill, or action over and over again. It is the kind of strategy we would use to remember an address or learn to do a lay-up in basketball. Rote rehearsal is most effective for learning a motor skill like typing or riding a bicycle when one wants the skill to become an automatic and almost unconscious action. Unfortunately, rote rehearsal is not as reliable for many of the things that are taught in school. Much of the curriculum of most schools focuses on information that would be contained in semantic memory—the memory of factual information, abstractions, things, words, concepts, and complex ideas. Repeating such information over and over again (i.e., memorization) may allow the learner to retain the information for a short time, but rarely will place it into long-term memory—the evidence that it has been truly learned.

> Elaborative rehearsal strategies are designed to enhance understanding and retention of the information by the learner.

Elaborative Rehearsal Strategies

To learn many of the things we need to in school (semantic memory), the second type of rehearsal strategy (elaborative) is much more effective. Elaborative rehearsal refers to a wide variety of strategies that will, in the words of Wolfe (2001), "encourage the learner to elaborate on the information in a manner that enhances understanding and retention of the information" (p. 102). The goal is to give the information meaning and relevance. The best elaborative rehearsal strategies are ones that are whole brain, activating both hemispheres of the brain and utilizing a number of different memory pathways. Often these will include using visual, artistic, and creative techniques integrated with reading and writing tasks. Other techniques involve incorporating movement, music, and/or rhythm, and ample opportunities for discussion and dialogue. Students should also be presented with opportunities for individual, small group, and whole-class activities. Elaborative rehearsal strategies can and should include a wide variety of instructional strategies and approaches.

WHAT POWERFUL IDEA # 5 MEANS FOR TEACHERS: USING MULTIPLE MEMORY PATHWAYS

Teachers need to teach in such ways (i.e., orchestrate learning experiences) that will establish many different types of memory pathways. In particular, teachers need to embed learning experiences in relevant, real life, hands-on activities where episodic and procedural memories can be developed and where the brain has better opportunities to create the patterns and neural pathways that will connect prior learning with the new. Semantic information is better taught in an integrated contextual way and not in a disconnected isolated fashion. Teachers need to recognize that, in order for students to learn most new things, students will need many opportunities to process information through review and rehearsal. Students need to be able to reflect upon what they have learned and connect it with what they already know so that the new information can be effectively integrated with and consolidated into what they have previously learned. For much of what we require students to learn in schools, this means using a variety of elaborative rehearsal strategies. It is very rare for anyone to learn semantic information after only one attempt. Anne Davis (2000) has written that "doing things more than once is essential for learning . . . It is when (students) do something the second and third [and fourth and fifth, etc.] time that they learn *what they know* and *what they need to know* [italics added]. Students need practice to learn" (p. 5). Most students will require a number of different rehearsal strategies to develop the complete understanding that we want the students to demonstrate. Simply teaching the new information once, in most situations, will not suffice. Figure 8.2 provides 12 excellent rehearsal strategies you can use with your students to help them develop deeper understanding.

"Doing things more than once is essential for learning"

Anne Davis, Making Classroom
Assessment Work, 2000, p. 5

Figure 8.2 Twelve Elaborative Rehearsal Strategies You Should Try

Strategy	A Brief Explanation
1. The Key Word or Phrase	Teacher supplies a key word or phrase about a particular topic or concept (e.g., water cycle or democracy). Students print the word or phrase in large letters vertically on the left side of a standard page and then must write a phrase beginning with each letter to the right of that letter. Each phrase conveys some understanding about the big idea or concept.
2. Piggyback Songs	Great ways to teach concepts and content in an entertaining way! Piggyback songs use a familiar song or melody to which are written lyrics that teach specific content and concepts (e.g., rock cycle). Students review content by singing song with partners or the class. Students often enjoy producing their own piggyback songs. Great assessment tool as well!
3. Kinesthetic Flow Charts or Diagrams	Can be used to introduce or review concept or idea. A concept that involves a sequence, stages, or steps to it (e.g., water cycle or steps in stages of growth) is mapped out on class room floor with large arrows and labels. Students move through the flow chart or diagram as teacher or another student reads a script that outlines the stages, steps, or phases.
4. Reciprocal Read and Teaching	Students work in pairs. Each student is given the same one page reading of some important content material. The reading is subdivided into an even amount of smaller readings (e.g., each paragraph). Each partner reads a section to a partner who must then paraphrase the readings and describe what it means to him or her. The process is reversed for the next section of reading. When the entire reading has been covered, the partners must then summarize the entire reading using some graphic organizer.
5. One-minute Commercial or Public Service Announcement (PSA)	After learning some new concept or idea, student groups are given the task of scripting, rehearsing, and eventually presenting to class a one-minute commercial or PSA that summarizes the concept just learned. Students should be given only 10 to 15 minutes so that it is more spontaneous and immediate in impact.
6. Physical Modeling	Students physically model or role-play a concept or idea (e.g., the motion of water molecules in solid, liquid, gas or the movement of the earth around sun to demonstrate seasons).
7. Learning Partners and One-Minute Reviews	All students are assigned learning partners and at various times throughout class, teacher says, "Find your learning partner" and provides a prompt or question for the partners to discuss for one minute (e.g., Find your learning partner and tell him or her what we have just learned about push-and-pull migration factors).
8. Roving Investigators	One half of the class is given brief information cards containing some new knowledge about the topic or subject being studied. The other half of the class are the roving investigators. Students are given a few minutes to become familiar with information on card or create some interview questions. The roving investigators must move about the class interviewing those with information cards and compile a short summary report about the topic. All the summary reports are shared with entire class. The procedure is then reversed with a new set of info cards on the same topic or subject.

Strategy	A Brief Explanation
9. Physical Timelines	Students are each given a card on which is written a particular event in a certain timeline (e.g., the events prior to and during the Civil War or the geological time scale). Along a properly portioned timeline (for example in the hallway or gymnasium), students must line up in the appropriate place. Really helps students see and appreciate the time distribution and length of events. Can also be used for such ideas as proportional spacing of bodies in solar system or numbers along a number line.
10. Mnemonics and Memory Aids	Mnemonics refer to a wide range of different memory aids that students can use to review important ideas and concepts. Includes such devices as *acrostic sentences* – a contrived sentence where each word reminds learner of some important aspect (e.g., Every Good Boy Deserves Fudge (notes on treble clef); *acronyms* – a single word or phrase that stands for a concept or idea (e.g. SCUBA – self-contained, underwater breathing apparatus); *key word or phrase* – (e.g., "Duck and Muck" – trench warfare in WWI); *body-pegging* – different parts of body are used to remind students of important ideas. There are lots of good references with other ideas, and students are wonderful at making up good memory devices if the teacher encourages them to do so. Make sure these are shared with all students.
11. Guided Visualization	In this strategy, the teacher asks students to close their eyes and imagine being part of a certain scenario or situation as she or he vividly describes it (e.g., the boredom, the wet and cold of trench warfare in WWI). After listening and imagining what the situation must have been like, students then write or sketch their impressions, ideas, or thoughts around the scenario using some prompt or reflection graphic organizer.
12. Looping (Bulla, 2000)	Looping is an excellent review strategy using a series of cards on which is written a question and an answer to another question about the topic being studied (e.g., geometry terms). Each student receives a card, and the review begins with one student asking his or her question (e.g., Who has the term for an angle that is exactly 90 degrees?). Another student will have the answer on his or her card and will reply, "I have right angle." Then he or she will ask the question written on his or her card. The looping review continues until all questions and answers have been given, and the loop ends up back at the original student who would have the answer to the last question asked on his or her card—hence, the loop. This strategy works particularly well if, after modeling it several times in class, the teacher asks students to compose their own series of looping cards for the class. It offers several opportunities for students to review important ideas, concepts, or terms.

HOW IT MIGHT LOOK—A CASE STUDY

Mrs. Singh's Musical Science

Mrs. Singh has discovered that using raps and songs has greatly increased her students' understanding of many of the scientific concepts she teaches and, in particular, has helped to reinforce their use of the appropriate scientific vocabulary and terminology. She has designed a number of songs and raps to teach such concepts as particle theory, the water cycle, molecular theory, plate tectonics, the rock cycle, and human physiology, to name but a few. Her students particularly like it when she adds physical movements or rhythmic motions that relate to or convey the idea of the concept. One of the favorites is a song with simple dance movements called the "Bump and Grind" that explains plate tectonics. Mrs. Singh often creates piggyback songs to help students remember important scientific concepts. Piggyback songs use a very familiar tune or melody to which Mrs. Singh adds new lyrics to explain the scientific idea or terminology. Mrs. Singh also has discovered that there is a rich source of other raps, songs, and jingles available on the Internet and has developed quite a collection to use for a large number of science topics. She also encourages her students to demonstrate their understanding of particular scientific ideas, process, or concepts by writing and performing their own original songs and raps.

9

Powerful Idea #6

Physical Activity and Movement

EXERCISE FOR THE BRAIN

Physical activity and movement greatly enhance learning for the teenage brain. There is no longer any doubt of the powerful link between physical activity and learning. A number of key connections and relationships between learning and physical activity have been identified. A recent study at the University of Illinois, reported in the *Chicago Tribune*, quoted Arthur Kramer, one of the researchers: "What our data show is that you can actually enhance cognition and brain structure and function. Exercise helps build the brain" (cited in Kotulak, 2004, p. 7). Regular exercise was shown to increase neural connections in parts of the brain and increase attention, and appeared to aid problem solving and memory retention. Such findings are of particular significance for the developing teenage brain.

> The brain requires over 20% of the body's blood flow, oxygen, and nutrition.

Our brain, even though it is only about 3% of the body's volume and mass, requires over 20% of the body's blood flow, oxygen, and nutrition. Frequent exercise ensures that the brain receives these vital supplies with the regularity that it requires. Physical activity also plays a role in regulating the energy cycles of the brain and the production of hormones. The brain has a cyclical nature to its energy and attention levels, alternately rotating through degrees of high and low energy. Physical activity assists in adjusting and regulating these energy and attention cycles, smoothing them out. Exercise can also literally wake up the brain by ensuring that both hemispheres of the brain are activated and that learning becomes more of a whole-brain experience. Brain scans have shown that in times of stress, threat, and anxiety, the brain triggers the release of stress hormones into the blood stream to prepare the body for the fight-or-flight response. Physical activity helps regulate and adjust the amounts of these stress hormones and ensures that these chemicals do not reach damaging levels. This is of particular application to the teenage learner. Since mood control and emotional balance is such a delicate and often unpredictable aspect of teenage life, teachers need some reliable strategy that can help regulate their students' emotional states. Physical activity can provide this. Exercise has also been shown to trigger the release of the hormone endorphin—a hormone associated with a sense of well being that is conducive to establishing the appropriate mental and emotional state for learning. A study at the University of California (Jensen, 1998b) discovered that physical activity caused the release of brain-derived neurotrophic factor (BDNF), a chemical shown to enhance cognition by increasing the synaptic communication between neurons.

> **Physical activity helps regulate and control the levels of potentially damaging stress hormones in the adolescent brain!**

For the developing adolescent brain, physical activity is especially important. Physical activity has been shown to influence the development of two extremely vital areas in the evolving teenage brain—the cerebellum and the hippocampus. Readers will recall that the cerebellum is an area at the rear base of the brain that is largely responsible for the control and coordination of basic muscle movements and motor skills. Neuroscientists feel it may also have a significant role in the regulation of higher-level thought processes like decision making and prioritizing information. It seems likely that if teenagers are more physically active, then this vital part of the brain will have a better chance to develop to its fullest. This can only help with both the teenager's physical and cognitive development. Since the cerebellum has been shown to continue to grow and develop well into the twenties, physical activity should be a key component of learning experiences for all adolescents whether 13 or 19 years old.

> **Physical activity is essential to the full development of several vital areas of the adolescent brain!**

The hippocampus, an area of the brain critical in memory formation, is another area where the growth of neural pathways has been linked to and shown to be influenced by physical activity. Regular physical activity during the adolescent years could have very significant effects on optimizing the development of this important area of the brain. Studies (Gabriel, 2001) at the Salk Institute in California have shown that exercise apparently increases the development and survival rate of new cells in the hippocampus.

Many learners prefer tactile and kinesthetic modes of learning—that is, they need the hands-on, physical connections and associations to effectively learn. Using physical activity and movement exercises greatly facilitate the learning of these students. Physical activity significantly impacts memory for all learners. Information learned through sensory motor skills (referred to as Implicit—procedural memory) forms more permanent memory pathways and can be recalled and utilized more easily. In other words, learning through procedural memory (physical connections) is more effective in the long run and produces better long-term recall. Recent studies at the Institute of Cognitive Neuroscience at University College London (cited in Radford, 2004) suggest that movement memory pathways may be so strong in some individuals (dancers, professional athletes) that the brain can simulate the skill without actual physical movement and individuals can reinforce the memory pathway by merely observing or mentally rehearsing the motion. All of this important research strongly suggests that there are many important reasons to include physical activity in secondary classrooms (see Figure 9.1).

Figure 9.1   Eight Good Reasons to Use Physical Activity and Movement in Secondary Classrooms

- Physical activity regulates energy and attention levels in the brain and affects the release of hormones that either impede or enhance learning.
- Physical activity can actually build brain cells.
- Physical activity optimizes the development of key areas of the brain like the cerebellum and hippocampus.
- Physical activity builds strong memory pathways that are more easily recalled.
- Learners become more receptive to and engaged in the learning experience.
- Physical activity and movement can provide the repetition and rehearsal necessary to place information into long-term memory.
- Many learners in the classroom are bodily—kinesthetic and tactile—learners.
- It is an effective and easy way to teach conceptual understanding and factual information to a wide range of learners.

WHAT POWERFUL IDEA # 6 MEANS FOR TEACHERS: UTILIZING PHYSICAL ACTIVITY TO ENHANCE LEARNING

Teachers need to utilize physical activity, bodily/kinesthetic, and movement experiences in their classrooms as much as possible. This is perhaps the one change that teachers could make to their teaching repertoire that would have the most immediate impact on the effectiveness of their teaching and subsequently their students' learning. Physical activity and movement might be considered the ultimate whole-brain teaching strategy because movement has been shown to be the one thing that tends to engage the brains of all learners and activate both sides of the brain. Physical activity significantly enhances memory and recall and, for many learners, represents one of the best ways of accessing information and processing sensory input. For teenagers, physical activity and movement can often provide the critical emotional engagement so necessary for motivation and attention to the learning task. Physical activity and movement experiences need to be a part of all classrooms at all age levels, but is particularly essential for adolescents. Figure 9.2 provides some ways that teachers can do this.

Figure 9.2   Making Your Classroom More Physically Active

- Use lots of activators, energizers, and physical breaks.
- Use kinesthetic models to explain and teach key concepts.
- Use lots of games, simulations, role playing, drama, mime, and physical representations in the classroom.
- Integrate and use physical activities and movement to teach content and factual information.
- Teach students to use physical actions or cues as memory aids.
- Make the learning hands-on and experiential whenever possible.
- Encourage students to demonstrate their learning (i.e., assessment) in physical ways (e.g., performance assessment).
- Encourage students to be active generally.

HOW IT MIGHT LOOK—A CASE STUDY

Kinesthetic Learning in High School Biology

As you read the following case study, consider the following questions:

1. Why do you think this particular instructional approach might be so effective in creating greater understanding?

2. How does the teacher integrate physical activity with other teaching strategies like writing and drawing?

3. How might Mr. Jensen assess how successful his students were in learning about the circulatory system?

The students in Mr. Jensen's high school biology class are studying the human body and body systems. While learning about the circulatory system, Mr. Jensen takes his class to the multipurpose room where, at one end of the room, he has drawn and mapped out on the floor large diagrams of the human heart and lungs and the connecting circulatory system. As he reads a script describing how blood is pumped through the heart and circulatory system to the lungs where oxygen and CO_2 is exchanged, the students must move around the large diagram of the heart and lungs mapped out on the floor. As they do so, they pick up red or blue index cards representing oxygenated blood or blood carrying CO_2 at the appropriate places in the circulatory system. After repeating this procedure several times, groups of three to four students are sent to the other end of the multipurpose room where each group is required to take a large sheet of chart paper and colored markers to diagram and label what they have just learned. After completing their own chart paper diagram, each group returns to the large map on the floor and walks through it again to correct any errors or omissions from their diagrams. Finally, using their own chart paper diagram as a guide, each student constructs his or her own copy on standard sized paper to use for future reference.

10

Powerful Idea #7

Memory, Learning, and Emotion

TOO MUCH OR TOO LITTLE?

Memory and learning in the teenage brain can be significantly affected by emotion. The impact of emotion on learning is figuratively two sides of the same coin—often a case of too much or too little. Excessively high levels of emotion and the wrong kinds of emotion will derail learning and make it virtually impossible; yet no learning occurs without the brain being emotionally engaged to some extent. How do we strike the appropriate balance—particularly in those highly emotionally charged and volatile teenage brains? For those of us who deal with adolescent learners, emotional balance may be the one aspect that most impacts their learning, yet it is frequently the one thing that many teachers neglect to consider or deal with in an appropriate manner. We have seen that the part of the brain—the frontal cortex—that controls and influences rational decision making and self-control is only slowly developing in teenagers. Brain scans have shown that most teenagers process emotional information or sensory data that has a high emotional context in that part of the brain called the amygdala rather than in the frontal cortex as adults do. The amygdala is the part of the brain where more primitive emotional reactions like strong anger, fear, or the fight-or-flight response takes place. The consequence is that most teenagers often misread the emotional environment around them or the emotional signals received from others causing them to overreact, make poor decisions, or generally respond inappropriately. Many neuroscientists who study adolescents refer to this as "thinking with their amygdala." This is particularly true during early adolescence.

Dr. Francine Benes, professor of psychiatry and neurology at Harvard Medical School (cited in Strauch, 2003) points out that during "early adolescence emotional experiences are not very well integrated with cognitive processes. That means you may get an impulsive action that seems to bear little relation to what is otherwise happening" (p. 54). Educators need to become much more aware of the role of emotion in influencing and controlling the receptiveness of the teenage brain to new learning. Teachers must develop a greater understanding of the role of emotion in three interconnected aspects of cognitive processing in the adolescent brain. These include the impact of high stress and threat on memory and learning, the role of emotion in brain attention and focus, and finally, the relationship of emotion in motivating and engaging the brain of the learner.

> Most teenagers misread the emotional environment and signals around them causing them to overreact, make poor decisions, or respond inappropriately.

THE IMPACT OF HIGH STRESS AND THREAT

"Stress makes you stupid!" This phrase is often attributed to Daniel Goleman (1995), author of the extremely popular text, *Emotional Intelligence: Why It Can Matter More Than IQ*, who has used this dramatic quote to emphasize to his workshop audiences how significantly emotional stress can impact learning. The brain is biologically programmed for survival; and in an evolutionary sense, it is wired to pay attention first to sensory information that has a strong emotional content or that the brain perceives as threat. The brain cannot really distinguish between actual physical threat and emotional threat or stress, so it essentially responds to all threat and stress as physical threats. When the brain receives sensory information that it interprets as threat, this information is processed immediately; and the processing of other sensory information is stalled or is judged to be of lesser importance. As the brain attends to this threat, emotional data takes on a much greater priority; and more complex cognitive and cerebral functioning is given considerably lower priority. Strong emotional responses like anger, fear, and intense anxiety can override conscious thought processing. Some writers (Caine & Caine, 1994; Hart, 1998) have referred to this process as "downshifting," where the main sensory processing in the brain is shifted to the more primitive limbic system (the emotional center) of the brain away from the more evolved cerebral part of the brain.

"Stress makes you stupid!"

Attributed to Daniel Goleman,
Emotional Intelligence:
Why It Can Matter More Than IQ, *1995*

When the brain perceives threat or danger, it signals the body to release certain chemicals and neurotransmitters to deal with that perceived threat. For example, epinephrine (adrenaline) is released to stimulate the heart, increase blood pressure, channel blood flow to the larger muscles of the body, and generally prepare the body for the fight-or-flight response to the threat. Shortly thereafter, adrenal glands in the body are signaled to release cortisol to help balance out the body's chemistry and secretion of the other threat-induced chemicals. If the threat goes away or the body is able to use its big muscles to respond appropriately—that is, run away or fight back—these threat-induced chemicals are used up and their production stops. However if the brain continues to perceive a threat without the opportunity to disperse these stress hormones, there can be serious consequences. For example, if a person is under frequent and constant emotional stress, the brain signals the body to continually release these stress hormones. Long-term secretion of such stress hormones—in particular cortisol— can have serious effects on the brain. Cortisol has been shown to cause deterioration in the hippocampus—the area of the brain that is essential for memory and learning. Research from McGill University in Montreal confirms that "the brains of regularly stressed-out adults . . . exhibited a smaller hippocampus" (cited in Sokoloff, 2005, p. 3). Smaller hippocampuses have also been noted in teens who suffer from severe depression. Caine and Caine (1994) have referenced research that indicates that under chronic stress, the brain's short-term memory and ability to form new memories are significantly inhibited. These authors emphasize that we should be very concerned about the effects of long-term stress on students because not only does it have severe consequences for general health and physiological functioning, but also it inhibits cognitive functioning that impedes "our capacity to think, solve problems and perceive patterns" (Caine & Caine, 1994, p. 72). Those who teach teenagers should be even more concerned because some neuroscientists believe that adolescents overall have a greater sensitivity to and are generally more reactive to stress.

> The long-term secretion of stress hormones can have serious effects on the brain.

BRAIN ATTENTION AND FOCUS

It is difficult to separate learning and cognition from emotion. Both learning and meaning are strongly influenced by the emotional context of any learning event or experience. What people learn and to what degree is greatly influenced by and connected to their emotions, their state of mind, and such individual aspects as their expectations, personal bias, perceptions, and interactions with others. We tend to remember best those experiences that are dramatic, surprising, or have a strong emotional component to them. In fact, we frequently remember the context of an event or learning episode better than the actual content (Hughes, 1999, p. 25). Anything that captures a person's attention and engages the brain can potentially produce powerful and long-lasting learning. The emotional impact of a particular event, image, or idea appears to have a profound influence on placing it into long-term memory. Actually, emotional attachments appear to be necessary for three aspects of learning: the engagement of the learner in the learning task, the focusing of attention, and the formation of long-term memories.

> ## Anything that captures a person's attention and engages the brain can potentially produce powerful and long-lasting learning.

Effective learning appears to require the right state of mind—one in which the learner is fully engaged in the learning event and is focused on the learning task. It appears that the best learning climate emotionally is one that Caine and Caine (1994) terms "relaxed alertness." This occurs when the learner is in a state of general relaxation in a physical and emotional environment or situation that is low in threat and stress, but high in challenge. Challenge seems to be particularly important to engagement. No learning occurs without engagement. Things or experiences that are challenging, puzzling, surprising, or arouse curiosity cause the brain to become engaged and to begin to look for the patterns and connections that the brain is constantly seeking.

> ## Effective learning requires the right state of mind.

Focus or attention is equally important in the learning process. Emotional attachments dictate whether the brain will actually initially pay attention to the information it is receiving. Positive and productive emotional states encourage students to become engaged in the learning and to remain focused on the task. Novel, unexpected, dramatic, or sharply contrasting experiences not only engage the learner, but also keep the brain focused and attentive. Any information with a strong emotional component is a powerful attention-getter for the brain.

The emotional context plays a strong role in the formation of memories; in fact, it may be true that long-term memory is virtually impossible without emotional attachment. Certainly experiences or events with a strong emotional context appear to create stronger memory pathways that persist longer and are more easily retrieved. Although excessive emotional states created by threat, stress, or severe anxiety can greatly inhibit learning and thinking, no emotional attachment can be equally impairing. Even though the cerebral cortex is the area of higher-order thinking in the brain, its connections with the limbic system (the emotional center of the brain) is essential for learning and memory formation.

> The emotional context of any learning experience plays a strong role in the formation of memories.

MOTIVATION AND ENGAGEMENT

Motivation is an extremely important aspect of learning. A motivated individual learns more quickly and more effectively. Motivation affects the length of time that learners will dedicate to a particular learning task. If people cannot see the relevance of a particular learning task or activity, they almost certainly will not learn. All teachers want motivated students, but regrettably motivation is not something that teachers can "give" to students or insist that they bring to class. Motivation is highly personal and largely intrinsic, but there are things that teachers can do to establish the proper stage and state for learning. If this proper state and setting is established, motivated students are more likely the norm. The optimal environment appears to be one in which the learner feels safe, experiences low stress and little threat, has the freedom to take risks, and feels challenged or intellectually stimulated by the activities that are offered in that setting. Regrettably, it seems that many teenagers may be motivationally impaired. This seems to be due to the as yet underdeveloped area in the frontal cortex called the *nucleus accumbens,* a region of the brain that neuroscientists believe regulates and controls the reward-seeking mechanism that is so critical to intrinsic motivation (Wallis, 2004). Teenagers are notorious for living in the moment and having the need for almost instantaneous gratification. (This likely explains why teenagers are so attracted to video games, cell phones, MP3 players, and Internet chat rooms.) Consequently, secondary teachers often find and will need to recognize that it is important for them to provide more short-term extrinsic motivation for adolescent learners and have them focus on learning tasks and experiences that will provide them with more immediate and tangible rewards.

> Many teenagers appear to be motivationally impaired.

Alistair Smith (2002), in the text *The Brain's Behind It,* describes motivation as "a process that ties emotion to action" (p. 59). Motivation is largely an emotional reaction in which the learner sees benefit and reward in attending to the learning task or activity or anticipates some positive result or sense of emotional well being. This benefit or reward may be short term or long term. It may not necessarily be an actual tangible or physical benefit or reward. It could be something as simple as the satisfaction of completing a project, the pleasure of working with others, or the excitement of solving a difficult problem. The benefits or anticipated results that trigger motivation may be as diverse as the wide range of learners that we can expect in our classrooms. However, it appears that motivation in most learners is influenced by some or all of the factors listed in Figure 10.1.

Figure 10.1 Some Factors Which Influence Motivation in Learners

- Relevance
- Control and choice
- Challenge
- Social interaction—Chance to work with others
- Anticipated sense of success
- Need
- Novelty
- Cognitive dissonance or discrepant events

WHAT POWERFUL IDEA # 7 MEANS FOR TEACHERS: MANAGING THE EMOTIONAL ENVIRONMENT OF THE CLASSROOM

In a brain-compatible classroom, teachers must create and maintain a relaxed, safe, and caring emotional environment where stress is minimized, the sense of threat is diminished, and students are free to take risks and engage in challenging learning activities. It is important for teachers to recognize that when students do not understand something, it will cause emotional stress and anxiety. Helping all students to understand is really the key to providing a positive and productive environment in the classroom. Students should not be worried about embarrassment, ridicule, and fear of failure. Threat can never be used as a tool to try to motivate students. Teachers need to create a relaxed, nonthreatening, and stimulating atmosphere in their classrooms where both the physical and emotional needs of students can be met and where students can achieve the proper state for learning (i.e. relaxed alertness).

Teachers must recognize the importance of emotions in learning and memory. They need to utilize teaching experiences and instructional practices that provide an emotional context. Experiences such as role playing, simulations, experiential learning, solving real-life problems, performance assessment, and participating in community service education can significantly engage the learner and provide the emotional foundation for greater meaning and understanding. Providing learning activities that are novel or surprising, elicit curiosity, or offer challenges are excellent ways to gain attention, engage the learner, and develop and reinforce strong memory pathways.

Although motivation in learners is personal and largely internal, teachers can do much to make learners want to learn. We cannot expect students to come to our classes fully motivated to learn everything and anything that they are presented. Teachers must set the table by putting students in the proper mental and emotional state for learning. They do this by providing a classroom environment that is conducive to learning and by developing and implementing learning activities and experiences that provide motivation for students. Such learning activities and experiences need to include an effective emotional component and involve those factors (see Figure 10.1) that are known to have a strong link to motivation. Fortunately, there are numerous ways we can manage and influence the emotional environments in our classrooms and help students deal with negative feelings (see Figures 10.2 and 10.3).

HOW IT MIGHT LOOK—A CASE STUDY

The "Affirmative" Mr. Hawkes

As you read this case study, compile a quick summary (refer to Figure 10.2) of all the ways that Mr. Hawkes uses to create and reinforce a positive emotional environment in his classroom.

In Mr. Hawkes's classroom, the walls are decorated with an abundance of posters and charts that depict positive quotations from many historical persons about such things as perseverance, respect, good character, quality work, integrity, honesty, trustworthiness, and dependability. Mr. Hawkes has a large collection of these and regularly rotates them. He is fond of saying things like, "Remember as Madame Curie once said....." and "Mark Twain always said that...." Mr. Hawkes also has a number of T-shirts and certificates on which are printed some of these same positive quotations and regularly he will award one to a student for some unusual reason. "Today Natisha gets the Alfred Nobel award because she and I have the same warped sense of humor." Mr. Hawkes's students secretly know that these awards are often given out when someone needs a pick-me-up, and eventually everyone in the class will get one. In addition, Mr. Hawkes maintains a "Give Someone a Hand" box in which students are encouraged to anonymously submit the names of persons who deserve a round of applause for some contribution or other reason. Once a week Mr. Hawkes pulls out a name, and the class stands and gives that person a hand (even if he or she is not in the room!). Mr. Hawkes gives each recipient a certificate shaped like a hand to acknowledge that the class thought his or her contribution was worthy of "getting a hand."

Figure 10.2   Fifteen Strategies to Help You Manage and Influence the Emotional Environment in Your Classroom

1. Teach students about their emotional brains and some techniques that will help them recognize when they are perhaps overreacting as well as help them get back on track.

2. Teach students useful strategies for managing and resolving conflict in peaceful ways.

3. Use lots of affirmations and positive quotations in the classroom. Use such devices as team cheers, chants, or songs to create a "we are family" atmosphere in the classroom.

4. Help students get organized with such things as daily planners, personal calendars, notebooks, and personal bulletin boards. Assisting students with coordinating and managing the demands of their daily lives is a great way to diffuse a lot of the stress they can experience at this time in their lives.

5. Create advisory or mentoring programs in your school where students will have regular opportunities to discuss personal and school issues with an adult advisor or mentor.

6. Utilize lots of ways for students to diffuse or get rid of negative or unproductive emotions—for example, relaxation techniques, circle of friends, trash your troubles, self-reflection journals (see box on page 78).

7. Use physical activity, energizers, and stretching exercises as healthy ways to help students manage their emotional levels.

8. Create suggestion boxes or some other similar technique to allow students to comment upon or make suggestions about classroom approaches in a low-risk way.

9. Periodically monitor and assess students' feelings and attitudes about classroom practices and instructional strategies using nonidentifying approaches like anonymous surveys.

10. When giving students feedback or constructive criticism on their work, use what athletic coaches refer to as the sandwich method. In your discussion or feedback, sandwich the critical suggestions between two positive statements about the quality things or strong work that the student is doing.

11. Establish clear signposts and targets for student achievement. Discuss and develop with students the performance standards or evaluative criteria for various assessment tasks. Summarize in a clear rubric and post it in the classroom where all students can easily refer to it.

12. Use a variety of innovative ways to capture students' attention and get their minds engaged. Mystery and suspense are good ways to get students' attention. Such devices as thought-provoking visuals, controversial quotations, conflicting viewpoints, unusual fact sheets, cognitive dissonance, coming attractions, novelty items, or emotion-provoking music can be used very effectively to interest students in the new lesson, class, or unit of study.

13. Develop some system (certificates, T-shirts, quality performance cards, golden pen award, etc.) where you can periodically recognize the achievement and outstanding performance of students. Ensure that at some time all students are recognized for some achievement.

14. Create learning activities that have high, but generally positive emotional components to them (i.e., role playing, games, simulations, drama, field trips, improvisation).

15. Use music regularly to moderate and influence emotional levels in the classroom.

Note: These strategies can also be found in the glossary.

Figure 10.3 Three Good Strategies to Help Teenagers Diffuse Negative Feelings

Strategy	How It Works
1. Circle of Friends or Class Meetings	Circle of Friends is essentially a class meeting when at a certain time of day or week (e.g., a home base period), the class sits in a circle formation and any individual can discuss a personal, class, or school issue or problem and enlist the support and advice of the whole group. Norms and rules for operation are established at the beginning, and all participants agree to follow these norms and rules. Some teachers use the "First Nations" convention of a "talking stick" that is passed around the circle and the person holding the stick can talk and contribute. To be truly effective, a circle of friends meeting should be held routinely and on a regular basis.
2. Trash Your Troubles	A simple, but very effective method for helping students diffuse negative feelings. At the beginning of class, each student is asked to write on a piece of paper what is most bothering him or her and then crumble up the paper and throw it forcefully into the trash can, in effect "trashing their troubles." Students agree that at least for the remainder of that class, their troubles are in the garbage can.
3. Peer Mediation	Peer mediation is a program offered in many secondary schools where a group of specially trained students are available as peer mediators to arbitrate and help other students resolve conflict and anger issues. Such programs have been shown to decrease the amount of serious confrontations within the school and to help all students to become better at more peaceful conflict resolution.

Note: These strategies can also be found in the glossary.

11

Powerful Idea #8

Reflection and Self-Assessment

KNOWING ONESELF

Teenagers become more effective learners through reflection and self-assessment. Effective learners think about what they have learned and what it means to them. In fact, it seems that this is really what distinguishes effective learners from less effective ones. Effective learners are aware of a greater variety of thinking and problem-solving techniques and are able to reflect upon which ones work best for them and in what circumstances; they also know how to transfer these to other situations. This ability to examine the learning process provides these learners with a powerful tool for the consolidation and transfer of learning. Educational writers refer to this process of self-assessment, where learners can examine, summarize, synthesize, evaluate, and review their own learning, as *reflection* and *metacognition*. Caine and Caine (1997), in *Education on the Edge of Possibility*, conclude that true and long-lasting learning must involve "active processing" (p. 121) that allows "students to take charge of learning and the development of personal meanings" (p.122). This happens through "reflection and metacognitive activities" and "emphasizes self-reflection and deeper learning" (Caine & Caine, 1997, p. 122). Reflection and metacognition assist the brain in placing information into long-term memory.

> Effective learners think about what they
> have learned and what it means to them.

REFLECTION

Reflection refers to the process by which the learner looks at the learning process and at the information learned in order to "fix" the information and learning more securely in the brain. Reflection gives the brain the chance to sort, rearrange, and reconnect information so as to internalize the learning. Reflection allows the brain to essentially rewire its neural pathways as it connects and relates new information to the older ideas already in existence. Robin Fogarty (1998) asserts that reflection "drives personal application and transfer of learning. It makes learning personal, purposeful, meaningful, and relevant and gives the brain reason to pay attention, understand and remember" (p. 657). It is in this phase of learning that the transfer of learning happens. Transfer refers to that process where the learner can move beyond the mere acquisition of knowledge to generalization and application. It is the transfer of learning that really makes learning powerful and long-lasting. When teachers can foster the transfer of learning, they ensure that students will develop deep and personal meaning and genuine understanding.

> Metacognition is thinking about thinking.

METACOGNITION

Metacognition is frequently described as thinking about thinking. Bransford et al. (2000) describe metacognition as a learner's ability to predict his or her performance on various learning tasks and to monitor or evaluate his or her current levels of mastery and understanding (p. 12). Later in the text, the authors point out that "the ability to recognize the limits of one's current knowledge, then take steps to remedy the situation, is extremely important for learners of all ages" (Bransford et al., p. 47). Metacognition is really a way of providing descriptive feedback to oneself about one's own learning. Such self-assessment is vital to the sustainability of the learning. Metacognition is seen as not only enhancing the initial learning, but also reinforcing it so that the learner can apply it in the future to other situations and circumstances, thus the transfer of learning. Bransford et al. (2000) cite research that indicates that metacognitive teaching practices have been shown to increase the extent to which students can apply their learning to new situations (p. 12). Such metacognitive teaching chiefly emphasizes meaning-making, self-assessment, and reflection on what works and what needs improving. Most writers agree that although some students may know how to do this, they do so inconsistently. The majority of students need to be intentionally taught such metacognitive strategies.

WHAT POWERFUL IDEA # 8 MEANS FOR TEACHERS: DEVELOPING REFLECTIVE LEARNERS

Teenagers are not particularly good at reflection and self-assessment since this intellectual ability is just beginning to fully develop in their brains. Coupled with a high degree of emotional decision making and a teen's own uncertain and evolving self-identify, most adolescents find it very difficult to rationally self-assess their own learning and what works best for them. Yet this is one of the most important higher-level intellectual skills for them to develop. Consequently, teachers need to provide explicit instruction on reflection and metacognition strategies and give ample opportunities for their students to use these during the learning experience. Teachers need to provide time and encourage students to reflect upon their own learning processes and experiences. Figure 11.1 offers some strategies for developing more reflective learners.

Figure 11.1   Some Strategies to Help Develop More Reflective Learners

Use learning activities and experiences that ask students to generalize, apply, or transfer information and knowledge to other situations.

Provide ample opportunities for formative assessment and descriptive feedback during the learning process. Descriptive feedback provides specific, regular, and timely advice and information to learners during the learning process on what the learners have done well, what needs to be improved, and what the learner needs to do to reach learning goals.

Utilize graphic organizers and other such devices that require students to summarize, synthesize, and evaluate new learnings. For example, PMI (Positive, Minus, Most Interesting; de Bono, 1986), KWL (Know, Want to Know, Learned; Ogle, 1986), What? So What? Now What?, or Six Thinking Hats (de Bono,1985). For more information about these techniques, please refer to the glossary.

Develop sets of reflective or metacognitive questions that will prompt or engage students in thinking about their own learning. Examples: What was the most important thing you learned today in class? Why do you think so? What must I remember to do when I . . . ? What piece of learning will help you the most to . . . ?

Use authentic assessments like self and peer assessments, academic prompts, and performance assessments. Academic prompts are "open-ended questions or problems that require the student to think critically, not just recall knowledge, and then prepare a response, product, or performance" (Wiggins & McTighe, 1998, p. 14).

Teach students reflective questioning and encourage them to use them with one another during such activities as reciprocal teaching. Examples: What do you predict will happen next? Why did you think that? What evidence led you to think that?

AND! Reflect (do it out loud and share with your students) upon your own learning experiences and processes and challenge your own pedagogical beliefs and practices based upon this reflection.

HOW IT MIGHT LOOK—A CASE STUDY

Feedback and Reflection in the Visual Arts Class

After reading the following vignette, ask yourself what strategies Mr. Syme uses to help his students become more reflective learners.

Mr. Syme, the high school visual arts and design teacher, uses a project approach in his classes. His students are required to complete several art projects throughout the year, each demonstrating their understanding and interpretation of various artistic themes, concepts, and techniques. Mr. Syme has implemented two feedback schemes to provide constructive advice to the students as they progress through each project. One is an assessment and reflection sheet, which provides feedback in four categories: tips, targets, successes, and to think about. Tips provides some suggestions, hints, and cues; targets are things to aim for; successes are already strong and convincing elements; and to think about includes some possibilities and questions for the students to reflect upon. During each two-week period this feedback must be completed alternately through peer and teacher assessment. In addition, during the entire time dedicated to the project (usually six to eight weeks), Mr. Syme meets twice with each student in a 30-minute student-led conference. During these conferences, the students are asked to identify and reflect upon the strong elements of their work, how it conveys the various techniques and themes considered in class, and what they might do to strengthen its message and visual appeal. During this conference, Mr. Syme uses some probing questions to gauge the students' understanding of and appreciation for the particular artistic elements on which the project has focused. At the end of the conference, each student must identify (and describe why they think so) two different elements they believe represents their strongest work and the element they need to improve upon. Each student also receives a checklist that summarizes the key points, strengths, and observations of Mr. Syme.

Note: The four-category feedback strategy is modeled after an example in Hughes and Vass (2001).

12

Powerful Idea #9

Social Interaction and Learning

Teenagers learn best in a variety of social environments and social groupings. Teenagers generally are extremely social animals and value relationships and interpersonal interactions to a high degree. During adolescence, the interests, commitments, and loyalties of teenagers dramatically switch from their families to their peer groups; and their values, likes, dislikes, and ways of behaving reflect this significant change (Sylwester, 2003). An OECD report (2004, November) on the brain and learning noted that adolescents appear to "have an enhanced ability to learn social skills," and "there appears to be a window of opportunity at this age for social learning" (p. 13). It is an aspect of learning that has particular relevance for teachers who work with this group of students. Social interaction and collaboration are essential and integral components of brain-compatible teaching and learning. The human brain seems to learn best in social situations where it can experience talk and can compare and share ideas and information. Caine and Caine (1994) have noted that "one of our fundamental tasks as educators, therefore, is to better appreciate the social construction of knowledge" (p. 95). Although learning and the construction of meaning are highly personal and individual, there is no doubt that we learn from others as well. Learning is best thought of as a social activity. Marzano, Pickering, and Pollock (2001), in *Classroom Instruction That Works: Research-Based Strategies for Increasing Student Achievement*, have shown that organizing students into cooperative groupings, when done appropriately, can lead to significant increases in levels of achievement and learning in general. Figure 12.1 summarizes the views of four other educators on social interaction and learning.

Figure 12.1 What Four Other Writers Have Said About Social Interaction and Learning

"Collaboration is especially powerful in promoting conceptual learning, practice with creative problem-solving, the learning of language, and the improvement of oral communication" (Kovalik, 1994, p. 90).

"The brain develops better in concert with others. . . .a great deal of learning takes place by talking to each other—exchanging emotions and feeling, sharing, discussing, brainstorming and problem-solving" (Jensen, 1998a, p. 75).

"The brain's capabilities are enhanced by positive social interactions. . . .When you organize collaborative opportunities properly, you give single learners a great asset" (Kaufeldt, 1999, p. 59).

"Some research indicates that group problem solving is superior to individual problem solving, and that developmental changes in cognition can be from peer argumentation and peer interaction" (Bransford et al., 2000, p. 280).

A study by Ekwall and Shanker (1988) discovered that the more students are engaged in talk and sharing with others or are involved in directly teaching others, the more they learn (cited in Parry & Gregory, 1998). It appears that the opportunity to talk is a key route for the brain to learn. One can argue that teenagers need to talk and communicate with one another frequently and in a variety of ways to learn well. Because the brain responds immediately to feedback, interacting with other learners can help teenagers (and their brains!) reassess, review, and evaluate their own ideas in the context of what others think. This can help the brain to reexamine patterns and connections and form stronger neural pathways.

WHAT POWERFUL IDEA # 9 MEANS FOR TEACHERS: PROVIDING FOR SOCIAL INTERACTION AND COLLABORATION

Since learning is greatly enhanced by a social and collaborative environment, teachers need to ensure that they provide ample opportunities for learners to learn from and with each other. But teachers also need to recognize that at times teenagers will want and need to be by themselves and to work independently. This means providing a range of diverse social settings in which learners can learn individually and independently as well as interacting with and collaborating with other learners.

Eight Practices That Will Provide Social Interaction and Collaboration in Your Classroom

1. Provide lots of opportunities for students to participate in different student groupings and organizational structures from whole group to clusters, small groups, teams, and pairs.

2. Ensure that students also have opportunities for individual and independent work and self-reflection and self-assessment.

3. Teach students the appropriate protocols, techniques, and guidelines for successful cooperative and collaborative groups.

4. Utilize numerous grouping structures and activities that require students to share tasks, discuss, reflect upon, question, and evaluate information.

5. Plan learning experiences and assessment activities that require students to collaborate and share different group roles and responsibilities.

6. Provide ample opportunities for peer and reciprocal teaching.

7. Encourage a classroom environment where students feel free to talk, discuss, debate, and generally share their ideas, questions, and reflections.

8. Create a classroom environment where learning is seen as a shared responsibility and where all learners feel part of a larger learning community.

Instructional Structures for Shared Learning

It is essential that teachers structure learning experiences in such ways as to maximize the opportunities for students to interact, collaborate, and learn together. Numerous writers have developed and offered many suggestions as to the types and kinds of instructional structures that teachers might utilize. Generally students should have opportunities to work with learning partners, in small groups, and in the larger whole-class arrangements. Figure 12.2 describes six excellent organizational structures and arrangements that teachers should use. These and other shared learning structures are described in the glossary as well.

Figure 12.2 Six Instructional Structures to Increase Shared Learning in the Classroom

Instructional Structure	How It Works
1. Think-Pair-Share (Kagan, 1994)	Individual students think about a question or do a small task then pair with another learning partner to share ideas. Pairs then share in whole-class discussion.
2. Jigsaw Groups (Aronson, Blaney, Stephin, Sikes, & Snapp, 1978)	Four to five students begin in "home base" groups. Each student moves into expert groups where each new group becomes expert on some reading or other aspect of learning by discussing and sharing ideas within the group. Experts then move back to home base groups where each expert teaches, or shares, information from the other expert groups. This is usually followed by each home group completing an activity or assignment that requires information learned or acquired from all of the experts in each home group.
3. Inside and Outside Circles (Kagan, 1994)	All students within class are arranged into two circles—one inside the other. Students are paired facing each other so that the inside circle is facing outward and the outside circle inward. Teachers ask pairs of students to take 30 seconds to one minute to discuss or answer a question. Then one circle is asked to move to right or left two or three persons (or some other number). A new question is posed for new partners or the same question if it can have different responses. For example, What was the most important piece of information we learned today? Excellent review strategy and can be used by matching two learning groups.
4. Numbered Heads (Kagan, 1994)	Students work in teams or groups (three to five students) to answer a question, complete an activity, or create a response posed by the teacher. Team works to ensure that all group members can answer the question. Students are numbered within the groups and the teacher can call upon any team and any number within that team to share their answers with the class.
5. Group Investigations (Sharan & Sharan, 1992)	This is a more complex cooperative learning structure in which a group of students investigates a student-directed inquiry. Students identify an inquiry question around a certain topic suggested by teacher, develop a strategy for researching the question, collect information and carry out research, compile and tabulate their data or information, and then make a group presentation to the whole class about their findings.
6. Teams-Games-Tournament (DeVries & Edwards, 1973)	Similar to jigsawing, but usually used as a review or check of understanding. Students begin in home groups of three or four and review information previously learned. They then break into tournament groups composed of one member from three or four other home groups. Tournament group members then respond to questions usually presented on game cards where questions are written on front and answers are on the back. Each student keeps a record of his or her individual answers and is awarded points for each correct answer. Each tournament group completes a rotation of a certain number of questions or answers as many questions as possible in a certain time frame. Each member then returns to his or her home base groups and the score from each individual student is used to tabulate a cumulative score for the home group. The home group with the highest score receives some sort of recognition or acknowledgement as the winner.

HOW IT MIGHT LOOK—A CASE STUDY

A Jigsaw Activity in High School Political History

As you read the following case study, consider the following questions:

1. What main grouping strategy is Ms. Fairclough using?

2. What other strategies does she use to ensure more social interaction among her students?

3. How might you use these strategies in your class?

In Ms. Fairclough's Political History class, the students are examining the role and evolution of new political parties or movements and how these influence mainstream politics. The students begin in their home base groups by examining three questions Ms. Fairclough has posed for them: "How do new political parties or movements get started? What do you think are common features or characteristics of new political parties? How do new political parties attempt to influence the larger mainstream political agenda?" After some time for discussion and sharing by the home base groups, she calls upon the number two members of each group to quickly summarize the viewpoints for the whole class. The home groups subdivide and move into expert groups. In each of the expert groups, the students examine a case study that discusses a small political party or movement from the historical past and how successful it was in influencing mainstream politics of the day. Each of the students in the expert groups has a graphic organizer on which to record the group's collective ideas around the three original questions. After the allotted time in the expert groups, students return to their home groups and each student shares their information with the group. Each home group is required to design a large chart that will summarize the findings from the whole group. These are posted around the classroom, and all the students participate in a gallery walk to review each group's conclusions. In the gallery walk, the number three person in each home group stays by his or her group's chart and briefly explains that group's summary to the other groups as they move from chart to chart in the time allotted by Ms. Fairclough.

13

Powerful Idea #10

Time and Timing

WHEN IS THE BEST TIME?

Teenagers learn best at certain times of the class and after their brains have received lots of rest and quality sleep. Time and timing have a profound effect on learning. It appears that our brain does not learn equally well at all times either throughout the day or during our lifetime. Our brains are influenced by a number of different cycles and biorhythms, which affect learning, during our daily life and our life cycles. There are specific times—both during our lifetimes and during our waking hours—which present better or more optimal opportunities for the brain to learn. There appear to be better times during a person's life—particularly early childhood, and we now know, adolescence—to learn certain skills or kinds of learning. The areas of the brain, in which these skills and types of learning are centered, are more receptive to receiving this sensory input at different stages of the brain's development. The adolescent years appear to be one of those times when the brain is most receptive to certain kinds of learning and the development of important neural and memory pathways.

> Our brain does not learn equally well at all times either throughout the day or during our lifetime.

It seems that our brains are not at peak levels of energy and learning efficiency at all times. They go through a number of energy cycles that affect their attentiveness and their ability to concentrate and learn. We know as well that our brains are not particularly well suited to stay at a high level of attentiveness for long periods of time. The brain appears to need periods of rest. The brain apparently prefers to learn in a sort of alternating pulse pattern where a period of high focus is followed by a period of low energy, followed by high focus, followed by low energy, and so on. Time of day also affects the brain's ability to learn. Learners of different ages are more receptive to learning at different times of the day. The efficiency with which certain skills or modes of thinking are best learned can be dependent on time of day as well. Further adding to this complexity of time and learning are the daily switches in brain modality, where, even though most learners have a preferred left or right brain dominance, this dominance switches every 90 to 100 minutes or so throughout the day. In addition to those influencing cycles and biorhythms already noted, there is a number of other hormonal, lifetime, monthly, and even annual cycles that affect the brain's ability to learn. If one considers that each individual student in our classrooms—and the teacher as well—is being affected by these many brain cycles and rhythms, one can clearly see that this poses an immense challenge to the teacher to facilitate and orchestrate the learning in the classroom.

> ## The brain needs periods of rest and relaxation to be efficient.

AN OPTIMAL TIME TO LEARN

There appear to be a number of windows of opportunity for enhanced learning of certain skills and functions—language, motor skills, music, mathematical or spatial, reading—in a child's early years of development from birth to about 9 or 10 years (Sousa, 1999). Adolescence appears to be another critical time in brain growth and development—particularly in the aspects of emotional control, advanced motor skills (like learning to play golf), reasoning ability, and higher cognitive functioning. It appears that the dynamic growth and momentous changes that we now know are happening in the teenage brain make the teen brain particularly ready for great leaps in learning. However, because of the neuron pruning and myelination that occurs during this time, this heightened ability to learn certain skills and to establish potent memory pathways in such areas as language development, refined physical skills, and advanced cognitive skills may diminish significantly after adolescence. This research does not mean that people cannot learn these skills beyond these ages. But it does mean that at these ages, the brain is more receptive to these kinds of learning; and consequently, it is easier and more effective for people to learn these things at these critical times in their lives. This age dependent influence on learning has some very significant teaching implications for those who teach adolescents.

Adolescence appears to be a critical period in brain growth, development, and learning—particularly in areas of emotional control, advanced motor skills, reasoning ability, and higher cognitive functioning.

AN OPTIMAL TIME PATTERN FOR LEARNING

As reported earlier, the brain appears to alternate between periods of higher attention or focus and periods of inattention. Each period of time in the cycle approximates 20 to 25 minutes for most adults and is shorter in younger people. The length of focus and inattention time is roughly equivalent to the age of the learner plus or minus a couple of minutes. This means that for a student aged 14 years, the attention cycle would be in the order of 12 to 16 minutes. Some researchers (cited by Jensen, 1995, p. 56) have discovered that the brain seems to actually learn best when highly focused learning is interrupted by short periods of rest (2 to 5 minutes) or by switching to an activity where the new learning is applied and practiced.

Figure 13.1 Optimal Time Pattern for Learning

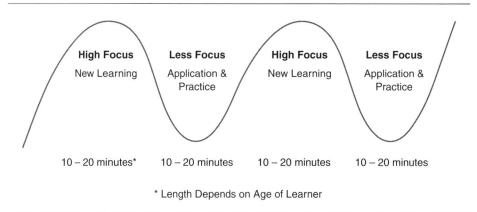

This time pattern influence is at best only an approximation of learning effectiveness. A number of other factors can and do influence a learner's attentiveness

The brain appears to alternate between periods of higher attention or focus and periods of inattention.

and time on task during a learning episode. Such factors as motivation, emotional engagement with the learning task, learning style of the learner, relevance to the learner, and even the physical environment can affect the brain's attention to learning. This is most true for teenagers who often require learning tasks that they find stimulating and motivating, include a high degree of personal relevancy for them, and which will show almost immediate and tangible benefits for the learning. This time pattern influence does tell us that it is unreasonable to expect learners to stay focused on a learning task, particularly if the method of delivery does not change, for extended periods of time. It speaks to our need as teachers to rotate instructional strategies on a regular basis, alternating between learning tasks that require a high degree of focus and those that require a lesser degree of concentration. For example, we might limit lectures to about 15 to 20 minutes and intersperse the lectures with physical rehearsals, application, and practice.

THE OPTIMAL TIMES
DURING THE LEARNING EPISODE

People learn more at the beginning and end of a learning experience than they do in the middle. This principle described by David Sousa (2006) is frequently referred to as the BEM Principle (Beginning-End-Middle) or the Primacy-Recency Effect. Sousa (2006) quoted research from several sources that illustrates that the learning and retention of information in any learning episode is time dependent. The prime or best time for learning occurs at the beginning of the learning experience, the second best time at the end, and the least useful time takes place in the middle. For example, in a 40-minute class period in school, we might expect the students to learn most effectively in the first 10 to 15 minutes, experience downtime for about 10 to 15 minutes, and then have a second effective learning phase for about 10 minutes at the end.

> The best times for learning are at the beginning and end of any learning episode.

Sousa (2006) also discovered that the retention of learning varies with the length of teaching or learning episode. The longer the learning episode is, the longer the downtime or nonretention time. Surprisingly the percentage of downtime to learning time as a percentage of the total time increased as the learning episode was lengthened. Sousa suggested that the optimal learning episode time is approximately 20 minutes. His solution to longer blocks of time (e.g., in semester high school courses) is to split the larger blocks of time into smaller units (about 20 minutes) within the larger time frame. One could take an 80-minute class and split it into four 20-minute miniclasses where you have a number of beginnings and endings.

Figure 13.2 The Primacy-Recency Effect

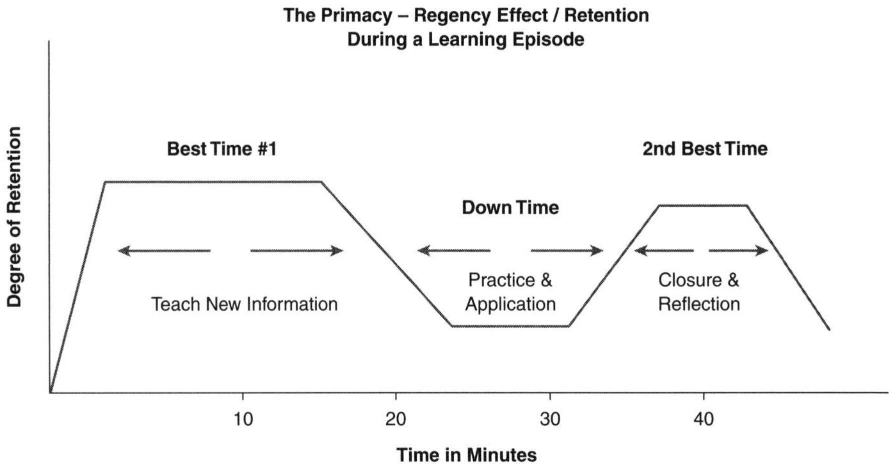

SOURCE: Sousa, D.A. (2006). *How the Brain Learns* (3rd ed.) Thousand Oaks, CA: Corwin Press. Reprinted by permission.

THE OPTIMAL TIMES DURING THE DAY

We do not learn equally well throughout the day. An internal biological cycle or internal clock called the circadian clock or circadian rhythm affects the times when we learn best throughout the day. Our circadian clock is dependent on a group of cells in the hypothalamus that go through a biochemical cycle of approximately 24 hours and that regulate daily cycles of waking and sleeping, brain activity, hormone production, and other bodily functions. Interestingly, this circadian clock changes at different times during our lifetime and can be thrown out of rhythm by such things as severe stress or sleep disorders. One of the most significant aspects of the circadian cycle is that it differs quite markedly between young children and adults and adolescents. The graph on page 93, adapted from Sousa (2006), compares the typical circadian cycles for both pre- and postadolescents with adolescents. It illustrates that adolescents have a slower and later arousal period in the morning, a later and less of a midday dip in brain activity, and a later but strikingly sharper decline in brain activity at the end of the waking day. This information has very clear implications for teaching effectiveness throughout the day and the length and timing of school-day schedules, particularly for those who teach teenagers.

Everyone who works with teenagers knows that teenagers are notorious for their late nights, their difficulty in getting up in the morning, and their sleeping in on the weekend. Most teenager's brains are not really fully alert until about 9:00 or 9:30 in the morning. This dramatic shift in the circadian cycle in adolescents and its incompatibility with the daily schedules of most teenagers typically results in what is becoming a chronic problem for many adolescents—insufficient sleep and/or disturbed sleep patterns. Because of their rapidly developing bodies and brains, teenagers actually require more sleep than what either younger children or adults typically need. The typical teenager should have between eight and nine hours of quality sleep each night, but most receive only about six and a half to seven hours. Various estimates have suggested that perhaps 70% or

Figure 13.3   The Circadian Rhythm

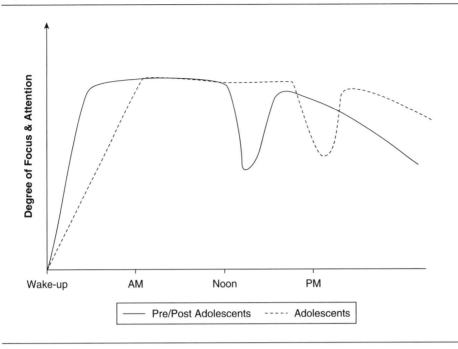

SOURCE: Sousa, D. A. (2006). *How the Brain Learns* (3rd ed.) Thousand Oaks, CA: Corwin Press.
Reprinted by permission.

more of teenagers suffer from sleep deprivation. Sleep deprivation has been
shown to have a very significant impact on learning and brain development during a critical period in these students' lives. Not only do teenagers not get enough
sleep, but also they are often missing out on a crucial phase of sleep (called REM
sleep) during which time memory and learning are reinforced and consolidated.
Sleep physiologist Mary Carskadon of Brown University (cited in Strauch, 2003)
has discovered that without enough REM sleep, people can become moody and
depressed and can exhibit memory and judgment impairment. They may also
perform poorly on reaction time tests. She also found that teens who get the least
sleep do the poorest academically.

> Sleep deprivation has been shown to have
> a very significant impact on learning and
> brain development.

WHAT POWERFUL IDEA # 10 MEANS FOR TEACHERS: TAKING ADVANTAGE OF TIME AND TIMING

Teachers need to be aware of the implications of time and timing in planning and
implementing effective instructional strategies for teenage students. Since the

brain is not equally receptive to learning at all times, we must, as educators, take advantage of the brain's natural cycles and rhythms of attention and activity to schedule and organize teaching and learning to maximize the effectiveness of any learning tasks or experiences. In particular, educators could and should pay attention to the strategies and considerations listed in Figure 13.4.

Figure 13.4   Strategies and Considerations for Taking Advantage of Time and Timing

- Secondary educators need to be particularly aware of and take advantage of the windows of opportunity for learning more advanced sensory motor and thinking skills during the adolescent years. These are critical and important years for experiences in physical education, music, art, drama, second languages, communication skills, and advanced mathematical thinking.

- Teachers need to ensure that learning activities are age appropriate. Students cannot learn things in areas where their brains have not developed sufficiently to comprehend and develop meaning in those areas.

- Teachers need to arrange daily and classroom schedules to take advantage of the circadian rhythm. For example, teaching more difficult concepts and ideas during the brain's period peaks and using down-time periods for consolidation, practice, and application.

- Student schedules should be rotated so that the same disciplines or subjects are not always scheduled during the same time each day.

- Testing and examinations should be arranged to take advantage of the brain's activity timetable.

- Teachers should break up lessons with other tasks or experiences that require a student's brain to shift gears—that is, use a different brain dominance, intelligence, or skill set.

- Teachers need to organize their teaching practices and strategies to take advantage of the natural pulse, or learning pattern, of the brain—that is, alternating activities that require high concentration with those that require less focus.

- Teachers need to organize their instructional time around the BEM, or Primacy-Recency Effect, to create the maximum learning advantage for their students.

- Teachers need to be aware of the brain's inability to concentrate and remain highly focused for long periods of time. Teaching methods need to be used accordingly.

- Large blocks of instructional time should be divided into smaller minilessons—for example, 60 minutes into three 20-minute segments.

- Teachers need to build lots of beginnings and endings into their instructional time since these are such powerful learning times.

- Physical breaks, energizers, relaxation pauses, brain rests, and movement activities need to be included in every daily schedule.

HOW IT MIGHT LOOK—A CASE STUDY

Mrs. Gregory's Lesson Planning

As you read this vignette, consider whether you could use a similar procedure to plan and organize your instruction to take advantage of the optimal times for your students to learn.

What aspects of timing in brain-compatible teaching and learning is Mrs. Gregory attempting to accommodate in her classes?

Mrs. Gregory has developed a useful time-saving procedure to plan her geography lessons in a brain-compatible way. She calls her method ACTR3 (Act the 3 R's)—A for Activation, C for context, T for teaching, and R for rehearsal, review, and reflection. She has created a recording template (Figure 13.5) on which are printed down the left margin the large letters A, C, T, R, R, R and a space for writing to the right of each letter. In her ideas binder, she has categories labeled the same way. Under A, for example, she has listed numerous examples of quick strategies she can use to activate prior knowledge; under C, strategies for setting the context of the lesson; under T, the main instructional and teaching strategies or activities she will use; under R for rehearsal, various ways students can apply and practice the new learning; under R for review, ways of reviewing and checking that students understand the newly learned material; and finally under the last R, strategies she can use to have the students reflect upon what they have learned. On a blank template, she writes in the activities and strategies she will use for each phase of the lesson or class providing some additional details on what specific information or concepts she will teach and what learning materials she will need to use. She also assigns approximate time allocations for each phase ensuring that she uses the BEM principle in her planning. Important concepts and ideas are introduced and taught in the first third of the class and then reviewed, reinforced, and reflected upon in the last 15 to 20 minutes of the class. The middle portion of the class, she uses for rehearsal and application activities. She also notes what modifications or adaptations she might need to make to meet the needs of all her students. She has found that this simple planning device has helped her considerably in ensuring that her lessons follow a brain-compatible sequence. Keeping a summary of all the lessons that she has planned and taught in this fashion throughout the term enables her to see which activities she has used, which have been most successful, whether she has provided the appropriate timing and balance, and whether she has thoroughly covered the subject material.

Figure 13.5 Mrs. Gregory's Lesson Planning Template

Lesson Phase	Teaching and Learning Activities, Experiences, or Opportunities	Time Allotted
A (Activation)		
C (Context)		
T (Teaching)		
R (Rehearsal)		
R (Review)		
R (Reflect)		

LOOKING BACK AT PART II— REFLECTION AND REVIEW

Targeting the Key Points!

- Learning must actively engage the brain and build upon what we already know.
- There are many dimensions to intelligence and different ways of learning.
- The brain needs to make connections and develop patterns in order to learn.
- Learning needs to be whole brain.
- There are different memory pathways in the brain and learning is enhanced when we can place information into a number of memory pathways.
- Learners need to rehearse and review their initial learning in order to place it into long-term memory.
- Physical activity and movement greatly facilitate learning.
- Emotion strongly affects learning.
- Reflection and self-assessment are essential parts of learning.
- Learning is a social and collaborative activity.
- Time and timing are extremely important to learning.

Some Questions to Ponder

What do these powerful ideas about the brain and learning mean for me, my students, and my teaching?

What do these ideas mean in terms of how I organize my classroom and facilitate learning in that classroom?

Are my teaching and assessment strategies consistent with and effective for the brain-compatible classroom and the teenage brain?

What do I need to do to create a more brain-compatible environment in my classroom?

PART III

The Classroom Environment and What Teachers and Students Should Be Doing

14

The Learning Environment

There is little doubt that the classroom environment has a tremendous impact on adolescent learning. To create a truly brain-compatible classroom for their teenage students, teachers not only must carefully consider their instructional strategies and teaching practices, but also need to attend to a number of other important factors that contribute to the total learning environment in their classrooms. The learning environment is best thought of as both the physical and emotional settings and conditions in which learning takes place. Regrettably, many teachers—caught up in the daily hustle and bustle of teaching—spend little time focusing on the learning environment in their classrooms and can become almost oblivious to the messages about learning that their classrooms can convey to students. All classroom environments have a direct impact on learning by affecting both the physical and emotional states of students. This happens regardless of whether the teacher is consciously aware of it or not or even concerned with it. This impact can be intentional and carefully orchestrated by the teacher, or it can be more subliminal and unintentional. Nonetheless, this physical and emotional climate will greatly influence the effectiveness of the learning that occurs. Many educational writers have referred to this as the hidden or indirect curriculum. Classroom environments should not be hidden or indirect at all, but rather need to be consciously and explicitly developed by the teacher if we want to ensure that teaching and learning occurs in a highly powerful and effective way.

> Classroom environments have a direct impact upon learning by affecting both the physical and emotional states of students.

Hughes and Vass (2001), in *Strategies for Closing the Learning Gap*, suggest that there are two key steps in creating the brain-compatible learning environment. The first step is to create an environment that **enables learning.** This means attending to all the physical conditions and material needs of students to allow them to learn optimally. Step two is to create an environment that **enhances learning**—an environment that stimulates, encourages, and invites learning and emphatically says that this is a good place to learn and that it is expected that all do learn in this place. Doug McPhee (1996) reinforces this view by stating that the learning environment is one of the eight keys to powerful learning. In his view, the learning environment needs to be functional and healthy and to demonstrate a secure and trusting relationship between teacher and students. The research of Martin Ford (1992) found that there are four essential factors necessary to achieving the most effective and motivating learning environment (cited in Jensen, 1995). Ford emphasizes that all four must be present to ensure optimal learning. First, the learning environment must offer a place or situations where learners believe they can reach their personal learning goals. Second, and equally important, is an environment that is consistent and compatible with the learners' social and cognitive learning styles. Third, the environment must also provide the necessary resources (materials, supplies, time, support, etc.) required by the learner. Finally, the optimal learning environment will offer a supportive and positive emotional climate in which there exists a sense of trust, acceptance, warmth, and safety. In a similar vein, Susan Kovalik (1994) maintains that the ideal learning environment—that is, a brain-compatible one—will be one in which eight elements are present: absence of threat, collaboration, an enriched environment, immediate feedback, meaningful content, choice, adequate time, and a way to achieve mastery of the things being studied.

> Classroom environments must both enable and enhance learning (Hughes & Vass, 2001).

From the work of these authors, we can see that the learning environment actually comprises several important interrelated components—the physical environment, the socioemotional environment, and the intellectual environment. It is quite clear that that to become a highly effective teacher and to create a genuinely brain-compatible classroom, one must attend to all three of these components to establish and sustain a learning environment that best supports teenage learners. We need to examine each of these three components in more detail.

Figure 14.1   The Three Environments of the Brain-Compatible Classroom

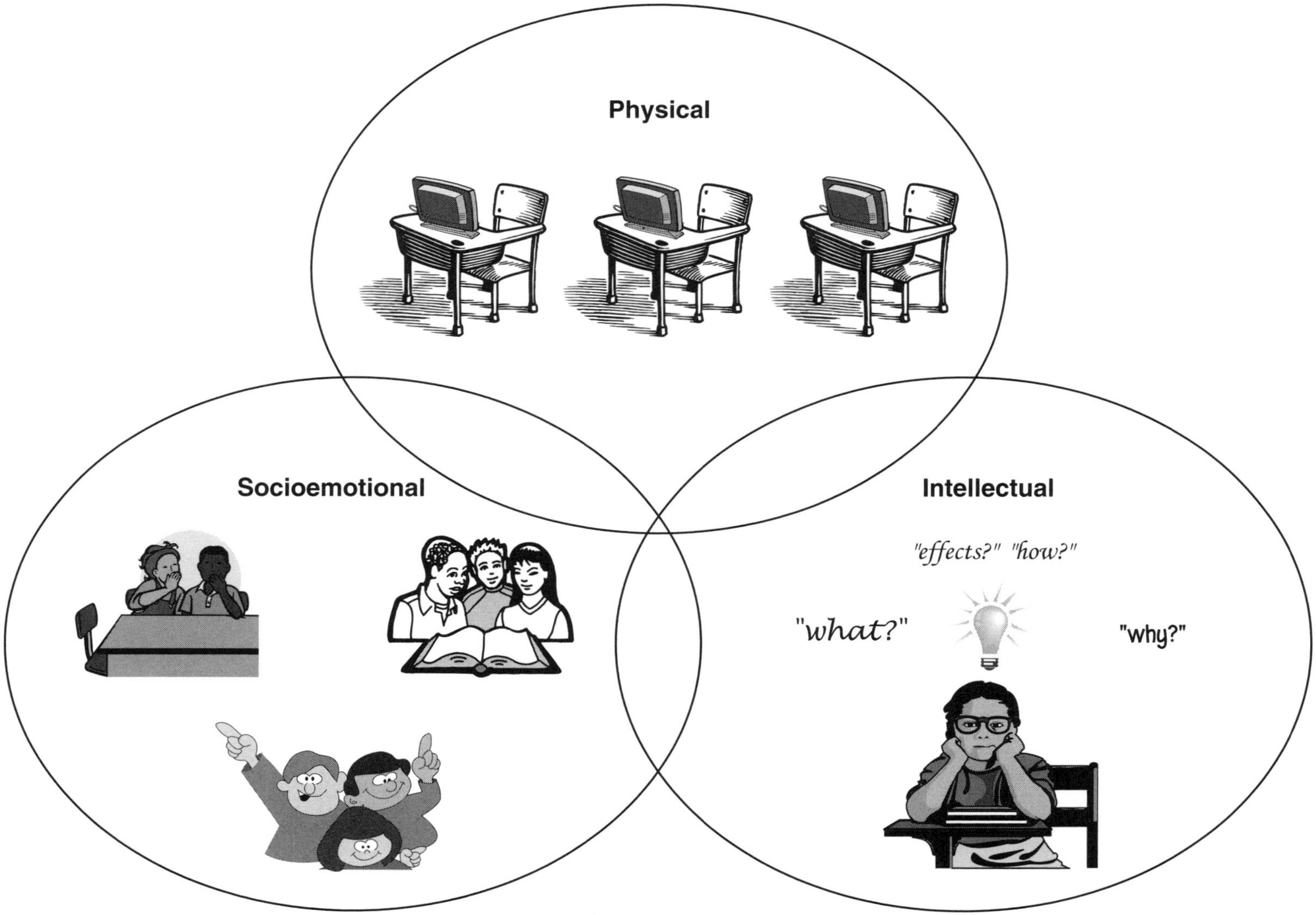

THE PHYSICAL ENVIRONMENT

It certainly is true that a well organized and resourced classroom, complete with attention to appropriate physical conditions and needs, does not necessarily guarantee a brain-compatible classroom and highly effective teaching. And while outstanding teaching can and does occur under less than ideal physical conditions, it is very clear that attending to the physical needs of learners and their learning space can immensely accentuate and enhance the effectiveness of their learning. We have already observed in the introduction to this chapter that the physical conditions of the learning space can greatly impact both the physical and emotional states of learners.

Unfortunately, teachers are frequently assigned classrooms and teaching areas over which they have, at least initially, minimal influence or control. However, my experiences both as classroom teacher and as a school administrator have shown that imaginative and determined teachers, given some small assistance and encouragement, can create wonderfully engaging, interesting, inviting, and highly functional teaching and learning areas. Often the secret lies in experimenting and making gradual changes, additions, and renovations to the classroom over a period of time. While there is no absolutely definitive list of physical requirements and attributes for the brain-compatible classroom area, there are a number of commonly agreed-upon elements and features that teachers should consider and attempt to incorporate into their classroom design and organization. Some will be more easily accomplished than others. Some, teachers will be able to do quite handily on their own, while others will require the intervention of school administration or even district management. One should think of the ideal physical setting of a brain-compatible classroom (see Figure 14.2) as an ongoing project, a work in progress, or an evolving goal towards which each teacher should strive.

Figure 14.2   Important Considerations to Making Your Classroom a Physically Inviting Teaching and Learning Environment

Moveable furniture that can be easily reorganized and can be used as individual student work areas or combined into larger work spaces. Individual small, flat-topped tables accompanied by comfortable chairs that fit easily under the tables are good choices. Student chairs should always be of the types that promote good posture and encourage face-to-face interaction.
An overall space that permits many types of movement activities and places for group learning. Ease of access in or out of the classroom, particularly for students who may have special needs. There should be more than one entry and exit route for security and safety. A variety of individual and group learning spaces of different sizes, shapes, and arrangements.
Workplaces for both passive and active learning—places for active engagement as well as places where students can do independent quiet work. Some living-room-type furniture and arrangements provide good spaces for students to read, reflect, and relax.

Figure 14.2 (Continued)

Spaces that provide a sense of security and safety with attention to proper heating, cooling, and ventilation. Spaces that have good lighting and in particular make good use of natural lighting or full spectrum lights. Lamps might be used for smaller areas.
Spaces that are free from toxic products (or processes) such as cleaners, highly perfumed products, or products that might contain such toxins or allergens like mold, dust, and dirt.
A source of or easy access to plentiful and safe drinking water.
Varied and frequently changed visual and tactile displays, posters, bulletin boards, and information centers. The brain receives a lot of information through peripheral sources.
Easy access to abundant and relevant technology and a portable sound or music system with a good supply of suitable and appropriate music.
A broad-based and varied multiresource class library appropriate to the subjects, topics, and disciplines being taught. These resources should address different interests, comprehension, and reading levels and as well provide for a full range of sensory materials—that is, audio, visual, print, graphic, and tactile.
Easily accessible and plentiful paper (different sizes, weights, colors, types), pens, pencils, markers, chart paper (and chart stands), and other such student supplies.

THE SOCIOEMOTIONAL ENVIRONMENT

> As educators, we need to find ways of decreasing threat, fear, anxiety, and mistrust and to create an environment where positive emotions provide a high level of motivation, engagement, and challenge for learners.

Because teenagers so frequently think with their amygdala, misinterpret emotional signs and signals, and generally feel everyone is looking at them, the socioemotional environment must receive special attention from secondary teachers. A number of educational writers have aptly described the appropriate socioemotional attributes of an effective brain-compatible classroom. Caine and Caine (1994) describe the ideal learning climate as one of "relaxed alertness" where the learner experiences a state of general relaxation, but is actively engaged in learning because of challenging activities. Such a physical and emotional environment exists when there is low threat, but high challenge. We have already seen that threat and high stress are very detrimental to learning and greatly inhibit it. Teens seem to be particularly susceptible to possible harmful effects of stress. We know, as well, that teenagers are frequently prone to feeling stress or threat (often even when none is intended!), so this aspect needs special consideration from teachers. Martha Kaufeldt (1999) emphasizes that teachers in brain-compatible classrooms need to "remove any elements or obstacles that might cause students to feel stressed, threatened, confused or anxious" (p. 21). Doug McPhee (1996) is equally emphatic on this point, insisting that a relaxed learning environment, where there is a healthy and secure relationship between teacher and students, is one of the keys to powerful learning. Susan Kovalik (1994) lists "absence of threat" as one of the eight essential elements of a brain-compatible environment (p. 10). Clearly what we need to do, as educators, is to find ways of decreasing threat, fear, anxiety, and mistrust and to create an environment where positive emotions provide a high level of motivation, engagement, and challenge for learners. This does not mean creating an environment that is emotionless or totally devoid of any stress of any type. Some types and levels of emotion and stress are actually necessary for learning. The secret lies in a healthy balance between emotional comfort and appropriate types and levels of stress. Positive stress—that is, challenge, curiosity, and the need to know—is necessary for learning. Without such stress and challenge, the brain becomes too relaxed and complacent and does not become attentive and actively engaged in the learning. Since teenagers often believe that nearly everyone around them is watching them and is as concerned with their thoughts and behaviors as they are; the challenge for educators is to create an environment where risk taking and trial and error are encouraged and where learners feel safe, but at the same time appropriate levels of stress and challenge spark interest and motivation.

> Positive stress—that is, challenge, curiosity, and the need to know—is necessary for learning.

Equally important to this atmosphere of relaxed alertness is the opportunity for learners to participate in a social and collaborative learning setting. According to Kovalik (1994), an environment that encourages and utilizes social collaboration as the main organizational framework for the learning is one of the key design elements of a genuinely brain-compatible classroom. From Powerful Idea #9, we learned that the human brain actually learns best in a social context and that learning is greatly enhanced through positive social and collaborative opportunities.

Thus our ideal learning environment for the teenage brain would be one where the teacher is able to facilitate an emotionally secure and nonthreatening climate in which relaxed alertness is the norm. At the same time, learners are eager to learn because the teacher provides interesting and challenging activities that give students the opportunity to work collaboratively with other learners in a variety of engaging and motivating experiences and arrangements. Figure 14.3 provides a number of suggestions to help create the appropriate socioemotional environment in the classroom.

Figure 14.3 Creating a Positive and Stimulating Socioemotional Environment in the Classroom

- Ensure that students associate positive emotions with learning through activities that utilize drama, music, novelty, affirmations, personal experiences, improvisation, and provide challenge.
- Validate and encourage the participation of all learners.
- Provide opportunities for students to learn about and use their own learning styles, preferences, and strengths.
- Provide ample opportunities for student choice and decision making.
- Provide students with safe and positive ways to diffuse negative emotions.
- Establish clearly understood procedures and opportunities to resolve conflict in positive ways.
- Use physical activity and movement to manage the emotional chemistry of students.
- Provide ample opportunities to celebrate learning.
- Establish clear procedures, rituals, routines, and expectations in the classroom. It is an excellent idea to have these prominently posted in the classroom as reminders and affirmations. Always phrase these in the affirmative. For example, in this classroom, "we do" rather than "do not" do this.
- Encourage a low-risk classroom environment where students feel free to share viewpoints, ideas, and diverse opinions.
- Use well established cooperative learning techniques and strategies.
- Utilize teaching strategies that force dialogue and sharing among students (e.g., Think-Pair-Share, Inside and Outside Circle, Reciprocal Teaching).
- Employ ample group interactive teaching experiences such as role playing, games, simulations, debate, and academic controversy.
- MORE student talk and engagement and LESS teacher talk!

THE INTELLECTUAL ENVIRONMENT

Two Key Principles

Two key learning principles need to prevail in the brain-compatible classroom:

1. Everyone can and is expected to learn in this classroom.

2. Learning is a shared responsibility. Everyone in this classroom has a role and responsibility in ensuring that everyone here can learn effectively.

Within each key principle are a number of important implications for the brain-compatible classroom:

Everyone Can and Is Expected to Learn in This Classroom

Educators must believe this above all else; otherwise our efforts become misguided and even fruitless. If the teacher is convinced of this, then he or she will continually convey this crucial message to the students. Once this idea is firmly established in the classroom, it then becomes vitally important that all students develop a strong sense of who they are as learners, their strengths and abilities, and how best to utilize these to become effective learners. Because teenagers are just beginning to be able to reflect upon their own thinking and learning and often have a heightened sense of self-consciousness, teachers will need to help their students in this journey of discovery. Students need to be taught about the uniqueness of each learner and that they all can and do learn. This means familiarizing students with what we know about learning and how best to use this knowledge to help all of us become better learners. It means specifically teaching students—consistent and appropriate with their ages and comprehension levels—about the brain and how we learn. It means helping students identify how each is unique as a learner and further assisting them with developing their own learner profiles in terms of multiple intelligences and learning preferences and styles so that they can come to recognize and appreciate their strengths and abilities and how best to utilize these. It also means explicitly teaching thinking and cognition skills and metacognition strategies and techniques. In these ways, teachers can assist their teenage students in the development and establishment of their own identities and sense of autonomy and belonging.

> **Students need to be taught about the uniqueness of each learner and that they all can and do learn.**

McPhee (1996) indicates that teachers need to cultivate both "intention" (p. 13) and "expectancy" (p. 21) in a powerful learning environment. If teachers want and expect quality learning and thinking in their classrooms, then they must act upon this intention by constantly seeking out and using new models for learning, thinking, and creativity in their classrooms. Students must come to expect that this classroom is about learning, thinking, and creativity and that all students will become active participants. Challenge, questioning, collaboration, and reflection will become the norm.

Once students have a positive perception of who they are as learners and that they are expected to be active participants in the learning process, then it is equally important for the teacher to set high but appropriate expectations and standards for learning. Research (McPhee, 1996) has shown, in a number of comparative studies, that students for whom high expectations were set and who were frequently reminded to perform at a high standard, did so. We have already seen that the brain responds to challenge and that setting such challenges in the classroom along with establishing the positive attitude that all students can and will meet these challenges does much to create an effective and vibrant learning environment. Hughes and Vass (2001) refer to this as keeping learning "high profile" (p. 22). Susan Kovalik (1994) stresses that teachers need to continually emphasize that all students must strive for their personal best rather than simply focus on grades or arbitrary achievement levels. She advocates the idea of mastery as a benchmark for success on any particular learning task, piece of work, or area of study. This, she suggests, is much more effective and motivating than the assignment of grades or marks.

Mastery occurs when work is judged to be complete, correct (i.e., accurate), and comprehensive for the level of the learner. By setting specific targets or standards for achievement, all students can obtain this mastery.

However, it is not sufficient for teachers to simply set the standards and then frequently remind students that they are expected to reach those standards. In the brain-compatible classroom, teachers have a much greater responsibility. They must create a culture of success and constantly convey the idea that they believe in their students and their abilities to reach those standards. This is particularly important for teenagers since adolescents often have such fragile self-images and frequently require almost constant reassurance and immediate rewards and feedback to convince them that they are capable of high levels of achievement. Most important, teachers must establish (preferably in collaboration with students) clear targets and benchmarks for success and show how it is possible to get there. Kaufeldt (1999) stresses that it is essential to keep students informed about what is going to happen and where they are going. This is done by providing continual feedback to students about their learning. For optimal learning, feedback needs to be **immediate, frequent, and positive in nature** (Hughes & Vass, 2001, p. 83). But most important, feedback needs to be specific and descriptive. Isolated grades or marks, nonspecific comments, or ambiguous suggestions (e.g., Try again!) do little to assist the student along the road to success. However, by providing ongoing, specific, and useful feedback, teachers can assist all students along the pathway to achieving developmentally appropriate expectations and standards. Hughes and Vass advocate using the language of success and possibility (i.e., **can do** language). We know that the brain associates positive experiences with positive affirming language. Using such language conveys a sense of success and the positive idea that the teacher strongly believes in the students and their abilities to achieve high standards and create quality work. Hughes and Vass maintain that it is equally important to remove the language of failure and blame and that teachers must, through their feedback, also acknowledge, recognize, and celebrate success.

> Feedback about student performance needs to be immediate, frequent, and positive in nature (Hughes & Vass, 2001, p. 83).

Learning Is a Shared Responsibility

Learning really needs to be seen as a symbiotic relationship among teacher, student, and all other students in the classroom where all the participants are receiving mutual benefits. This idea speaks to the highly social and collaborative nature of learning, but extends well beyond the simple idea that learning occurs best with others. Rather, it accentuates the idea that not only do we have a responsibility for our individual learning, but also we have a vital role and responsibility in the learning of others. We want our teenage learners to recognize and understand this critical role and responsibility. Equally important is the premise that I, as an individual learner, can become a more effective learner through my cooperation and collaboration with the other learners around me. In other words, my cooperation and collaboration will not only benefit others, but also is really essential for my own growth and development as a learner. Thus I have greater responsibility than merely my own learning. Students need to develop a knowledge of and empathy for the abilities, intelligences, and learning preferences of other students and how, by working with and drawing upon these diverse learners, their own learning is enhanced. Students need to come to accept that collaborative problem solving and creativity is not only the norm, but also the best way of ensuring that all students have learned and can meet the expectations of the learning task or activity. Perhaps the greatest responsibility of the individual learner lies in his or her contribution to creating an environment of intellectual trust and respect within the classroom. All students need to be able to feel valued as a learner—that their contributions are important and that they are free to act and respond to challenges and questions without fear of ridicule or embarrassment. This security to take intellectual risks must be paramount in the brain-compatible classroom.

> All students need to be able to feel valued as learners—that their contributions are important and that they are free to act and respond to challenges and questions without fear of ridicule or embarrassment.

It is obvious that virtually everything teachers say and do can greatly affect and influence the learning environment and the mental states of their students. If the teacher desires a climate where learning is kept in the forefront, where everyone is deemed to be a capable learner, and where expectations are high, the teacher must ensure that everything he or she says or does creates this positive climate for learning. This is a tremendously challenging role and responsibility, but one that is essential in the genuinely brain-compatible classroom. It represents quite a different role from the one traditionally assigned to classroom teachers, but one that will result in great benefits and satisfaction for both students and teacher when tackled with enthusiasm, humor, and affection.

> Virtually everything teachers say and do can greatly affect and influence the learning environment and the mental states of their students.

What specific strategies or practices can teachers employ to develop this creative and secure intellectual climate within the classroom? A number have already been mentioned in this section, but it is helpful to note these again, as well as to include several other useful ideas. The writers already cited in this section provide many interesting and effective suggestions to achieving this desirable intellectual climate. This abbreviated list (Figure 14.4) will serve as a good starting point for teachers.

Figure 14.4   Strategies or Practices to Develop a Creative and Secure Intellectual Climate

- Establish a climate of success—a can-do atmosphere in the classroom.
- Set high expectations for student learning and give frequent reminders of these expectations.
- Provide numerous and timely signposts and benchmarks to help students achieve high expectations.
- Develop collaboratively, with students, assessment and evaluation practices that will provide frequent and meaningful information about their learning.
- Involve students in their assessment and evaluation.
- Always use the language of success and possibility. (For example, "All students in this class will be able to . . ." "I know you can do this.")
- Avoid the language of failure and blame.
- Provide timely, positive, and descriptive feedback to learners.
- Help students identify and focus on personal learning goals and ways to achieve those goals.
- Utilize activities and create opportunities in the classroom that will promote curiosity and stimulate anticipation and excitement for learning.
- Keep students informed about their learning through such things as agendas, calendars, daily planners, timelines, or schedules.
- Create opportunities and assist students in developing their ability to analyze tasks and problems and make learning plans to complete tasks or solve the problems.
- Teach and model specific thinking and metacognition skills and techniques.
- Assist students in identifying and making personal connections to the curriculum.
- Provide a diverse range of learning situations from acquisition of new knowledge to application, synthesis, evaluation, and reflection.
- Post positive quotations, affirmations, lists of thinking or problem-solving strategies, and so on that speak to success around the classroom.
- Utilize questioning techniques that require students to develop deeper understanding (e.g., from the simpler Who? What? to Why? How Do We Know? Consequences? What If? Unexpected results? Significance?).
- Encourage students to use higher-level questioning in their own work or while collaborating with others.
- Utilize many strategies that require students to clarify or extend their ideas, concepts, or questions without fear of ridicule or embarrassment.
- Structure many opportunities for collaborative creativity—activities and tasks where the whole class or groups of students deal with a challenge or solve a problem.
- Teach, model, and require students to use various reflection techniques and strategies.
- Always demonstrate that you are a thinker and a learner too!

15

The Brain-
Compatible Teacher

Changing and Evolving Roles

A COMPLEX AND CHALLENGING PROFESSION!

> Teaching adolescents is a complex, multi-
> faceted, demanding, and challenging
> profession.

It must be obvious to readers by now that the role and responsibilities for the teacher in the brain-compatible classroom has to be quite different from the one traditionally ascribed to a teacher. Teaching adolescents is a complex, multifaceted, demanding, and challenging profession, but it is one that is vitally important for the success of all learners. I began this book with the premise that all teachers want to be effective in what they do and that they can become more so by developing a sound understanding of brain research, learning theory, and theories of intelligences and learning styles. This is the new science of learning. This new science of learning includes applying this enhanced understanding and appreciation of how students learn to the creation and use of pedagogical practices and instructional strategies that reflect and are consistent with this newly established knowledge base. This is what effective teachers do. Bennett and

Rolheiser (2001) point out that not only do effective teachers commonly have attributes and personal characteristics that are essential to creating a meaningful, safe, and respectful learning environment, but also they have extensive pedagogical knowledge and understanding about learners and learning. What characterizes really effective teachers is their ability to integrate these essential personal characteristics "with an extensive understanding of how students learn and an instructional repertoire that allows them to respond meaningfully to what is known about how and what students must learn" (Bennett & Rolheiser, 2001, p.11). Research by Marzano (1998) indicates that the degree to which teachers know and can apply their understanding of the teaching and learning process is one of the most powerful predictors of student success.

> *"Highly effective teachers are characterized by certain essential personal attributes integrated with an extensive understanding of how students learn and an instructional repertoire that allows them to respond meaningfully to what is known about how and what students must learn."*
>
> *Barrie Bennett and Carol Rolheiser,*
> Beyond Monet: The Artful Science of
> Instructional Integration, *2001, p. 11*

Bennett and Rolheiser (2001) describe effective teaching as a constantly creative process because teachers really have no other option. Faced with the myriad of variables and conditions that they often have little or no control over—social and home factors, students with disabilities and challenges, students with varying abilities and learning styles, externally imposed curricula, scheduling restrictions—teachers must respond creatively to meet these great challenges. Effective teachers accept and address these challenges by continually seeking new knowledge about their students and how they learn and through applying this new understanding to the creation of enhanced learning opportunities for their students. What this means, according to Bennett and Rolheiser, is

> the unequivocal implication . . . that we will improve learning when we collectively, intelligently, and creatively focus our efforts on improving the teaching and learning process. The more we understand about the learner, the more we understand about meaningful and responsible assessment and evaluation, the more we understand about what is to be learned, the more we understand about the instructional processes, and the more we understand about collectively acting on what we understand, then the more likely we are to make a difference. Teaching is a complex and creative undertaking. (p. 22)

Who could ask for a more thorough and apt description of brain-compatible teaching and the application of the new science of learning?

The traditional role of teachers, particularly in middle to high school, has often been seen as that of the expert at the front of the class, the holder and disseminator of knowledge, and the person who controls and directs all aspects of the teaching and learning. In the brain-compatible classroom, this role is considerably more diverse and takes on a whole different character and complexity. What are the different roles and responsibilities that the effective teacher in the brain-compatible classroom must assume? Here are five of the most important.

THE TEACHER AS FACILITATOR, ORCHESTRATOR, AND CONDUCTOR

This role is a multifaceted, but vitally important one. In this role, the teacher must take the main responsibility for organizing, facilitating, and stage managing the great variety of learning activities and experiences that will go on in his or her classroom. This means designing and selecting appropriate learning activities and tasks, obtaining and managing the resources and instructional materials necessary to complete the tasks, and generally organizing instruction and scaffolding learning experiences in ways that will ensure success for all learners. It means deciding upon and helping to facilitate individual, small group, and whole-class learning. It means attending closely to the various interactions between students and sometimes intervening or mediating when conflicts or problems arise. It means setting and organizing meaningful authentic real-world problems that students can work. Sometimes it will mean directing students to or providing them with information that will not solve the problems, but will help the students find solutions. It means giving clear and concise directions to students about the learning activities and tasks and defining the terms and conditions necessary to successfully complete these. It means guiding students through various types of activating, elaborative rehearsal, and assessment activities and experiences and helping them debrief and reflect upon these at the conclusion of these activities. Above all, teachers must move away from the position of perceived expert at the front of the class and as the central figure and focus of the learning.

THE TEACHER AS COACH AND MODEL

In this role, the teacher tries to move students to independence as learners, to guide them in their thinking, and to help them reach deeper levels of understanding. As coach and model, the teacher will portray and demonstrate specific thinking skills and applications of certain learning strategies to students; and through guided practice, the teacher will help them develop competency in using these skills and strategies. Specific feedback and encouragement from the teacher will help students achieve mastery of skills and reach mutually agreed-upon standards of performance. Regular conferencing between the teacher and the students will be routine and common practice. The teacher as coach has an important duty to recognize, acknowledge, and celebrate student

Figure 15.1 The Brain-Compatible Teacher

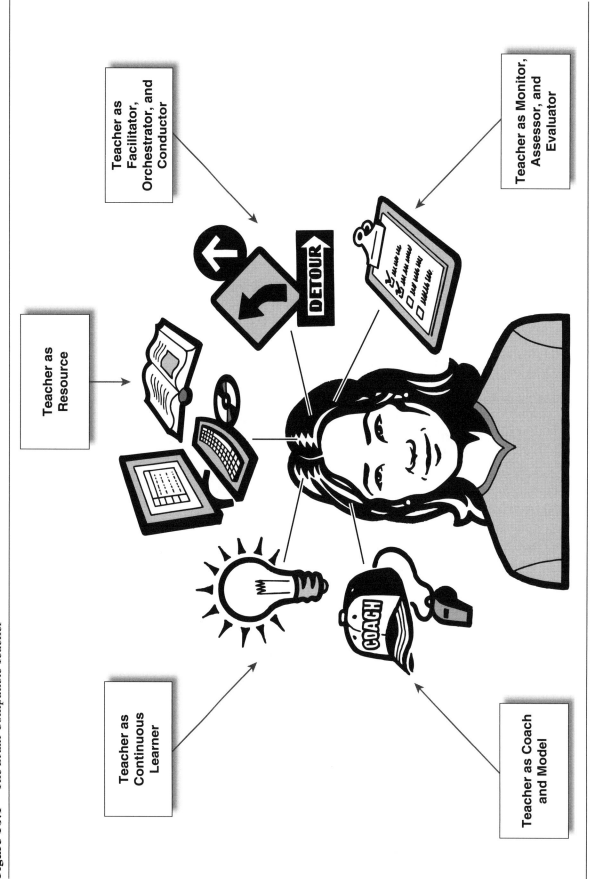

Teacher as Facilitator, Orchestrator, and Conductor

Teacher as Monitor, Assessor, and Evaluator

Teacher as Resource

Teacher as Continuous Learner

Teacher as Coach and Model

DETOUR

COACH

success. Sometimes the teacher will act as a copartner in the inquiry or investigation and at other times will try to point students in the directions that they will need to go to complete the learning task or solve a problem by providing clues or suggestions that will lead to discovery.

THE TEACHER AS CONTINUOUS LEARNER

It is essential that students see their teachers as active and continuous learners. In this role, teachers must constantly demonstrate a commitment to learning and show that they share many of the learning challenges and goals that their students do. Teachers should model different learning and cognitive techniques and should think out loud with their students about their own approaches to learning and problem solving. Teachers should describe to students and reflect upon their own learning plans and experiences. For example, teachers might indicate to their students that at the recent professional development day, they learned "such and such" and today they are going to try an activity that draws upon this new knowledge. As new activities are introduced in the classroom, the teacher should explain how he or she learned about these and what benefits he or she believes will occur because of this new understanding. The teacher should share with his or her students the ideas and knowledge gained through the teacher's access to and use of the latest professional books, journals, articles, and workshops. At times the teacher will need to be directly involved in researching the same issue, idea, or problem that the students are working.

THE TEACHER AS MONITOR, ASSESSOR, AND EVALUATOR

This of course has always been a role for teachers; but in the brain-compatible classroom, it has a greater complexity and serves a much more crucial function. Teachers must move beyond mere graders and markers. They need to develop a relationship with their students in which students become more involved in their own learning and where students learn how to gauge when and in what ways they have succeeded. The classroom must move away from the situation where students are merely replicating the information disseminated by the teacher and are scored on their ability to reproduce this information on a formal test. Assessment and evaluation needs to be seen as an ongoing process in which both teacher and students are monitoring how well things are going. Teachers must continuously look for the best match between instructional strategies and student success. They need to determine if the content and the expectations of the curriculum are appropriate and whether learning activities and strategies are effective in helping all students achieve success. Teachers must constantly remind students of the expectations, the signposts for success, and what needs to be done to achieve success on every learning activity or task. Providing timely, useful, and descriptive feedback to students about the learning is paramount. When formal evaluation and reporting of student progress is necessary, teachers work with students to determine the criteria and standards upon which success is judged and the types and formats of assessment that students could choose to demonstrate what they know and can do.

THE TEACHER AS A RESOURCE

This role is one that is closer to the traditional one. At times, the teacher will need to explicitly inform students about some strategy, body of knowledge, concept, or idea and may want to use a more traditional approach—for example, a minilecture. At other times, the teacher will need to set the context for a particular problem or activity by directly supplying background information or facilitating easy access to needed information (e.g., obtaining permission for students to visit a research center or by bringing in an outside expert). In some circumstances, students might go directly to the teacher to receive individual assistance or information to help them proceed with an activity. Generally students should come to see the teacher as one of many different resources that they might use and not as the sole holder of knowledge and the expert to whom they should always defer.

16

Teenage Students

Higher Expectations and New Roles

Regrettably in many secondary classrooms today, adolescent students are still doing things and learning in ways that have characterized classrooms for decades and that, unfortunately, have long been shown to be ineffective. Frequently, they continue to sit passively and with little interaction with other learners as the teacher gradually parcels out to them what the teacher believes to be worthy of knowing and in the form that is easiest for the teacher to transmit information quickly. The student is perceived as an empty vessel into which the teacher must pour as much information as is possible in the allotted time. The student has little choice in what is to be learned or in what way it is to be learned. Success is judged by the ability of the student to reproduce the information on a formal test assigned at the end of the learning stage.

> In many secondary classrooms today, adolescent students are still doing things and learning in ways that have characterized classrooms for decades and that, unfortunately, have long been shown to be ineffective.

Sousa (1995) laments that "lecture continues to be the most prevalent teaching mode in secondary and higher education, despite overwhelming evidence that it produces the lowest degree of retention for most learners" (p. 42).

Sousa's research shows that as students become more directly involved with their learning through discussion, rehearsal, practice, application, and by actually teaching others, their retention increases dramatically. In the brain-compatible classroom, students are interactive learners, engage in a wide variety of learning activities and experiences, and have considerable responsibility and input in their learning. Learning is seen as a shared responsibility between the teacher and the students.

WHAT WE WANT AND NEED FROM OUR TEENAGE STUDENTS

In this new pedagogical model, we clearly have greater and different aspirations and expectations for our teenage students. Ample research demonstrates that we no longer should be content to have our teenage students sit as passive empty containers into which we try to pour as much information as we can muster. Students must become active partners with us in the learning process. Figure 16.1 explains quite emphatically what we should expect and would want our teenage students to be doing in brain-compatible classrooms.

Figure 16.1   What We Want Our Teenage Students to Be Doing

- Participating actively with other students in a wide variety of collaborative and cooperative group learning activities.
- Resolving conflict and mediating disputes in positive ways.
- Researching and seeking information from many different sources and resources and evaluating, synthesizing, and applying this information, as well as their own experiences, to new learning situations or problems.
- Clearly exhibiting choices about their own learning and accepting responsibility for contributing to the learning of others.
- Responding to learning tasks in a wide variety of ways using different intelligences, abilities, and ways of communicating.
- Using opportunities to reflect upon their own and others' learning.
- Using a wide variety of assessment techniques and tools to demonstrate what they know and can do.
- Sometimes taking on the role of expert and teacher, particularly during opportunities for peer and reciprocal teaching.
- Using the whole range of communicative instruments and methods—speech, writing, drawing, movement, drama, dance, and the visual arts—to examine ideas and concepts, construct meaning, and convey their understanding.
- Frequently engaging in physically active learning and other forms of hands-on experiential learning.
- Participating in a number of integrated, holistic, and interdisciplinary learning opportunities.
- Participating in authentic, meaningful learning tasks and activities in which new learning and prior experiences and knowledge are applied to real-life situations.
- Working cooperatively and collaboratively with the teacher as partners in the pursuit of learning.

LOOKING BACK AT PART III—
REFLECTION AND REVIEW

Targeting the Key Points!

In the new science of teaching and learning (i.e., brain-compatible):

- Attention is given to the physical, socioemotional, and intellectual needs of learners.
- All students can and do learn.
- Learning is seen as a shared responsibility.
- Teachers have many different roles and responsibilities.
- Students are interactive learners and engage in a wide variety of learning activities and experiences.
- Students have considerable responsibility for their own learning and for the learning of others.

Some Questions to Ponder

To which components of a brain-compatible classroom do I need to give more attention?

How do I ensure that all students see themselves as learners?

In which roles and responsibilities of the brain-compatible teacher am I already most competent and comfortable? Which roles or responsibilities require more attention?

How do I involve my students more in their learning?

How do I develop a sense of shared responsibility and a community of learners in my classroom?

PART IV

Now What? So What?—Reflecting Upon What We Have Learned

17

What Does It All Mean?

"What does it all mean? In the end, it means that we shouldn't give up on any teenager, there is hope."

Jay Giedd, *cited in* The Primal Teen:
What the New Discoveries
About the Teenage Brain Tell Us About Our Kids
by Barbara Strauch, 2003, p. 203

You are probably reading this book because you are either a parent or teacher of teenagers, a secondary school administrator, or possibly a person who is responsible for the professional development of teachers who work with adolescents. As stated in the opening sentence, this book was written especially for those of us who work with, live with, teach, and otherwise associate with teenagers. Take a few minutes and reflect briefly on what you have learned as you have read this text. What thoughts did it trigger? What changes happened in your own brain as you read it? Was there an "Aha moment" when a particular piece of information suddenly made sense to you? Was there one defining idea or one particular notion that made you stop and think about what it means for you as you interact and work with teenagers? Did it provide new and useful insight into how teenagers think and learn? Or did it just confirm what you have always believed about teenagers and their brains? For those who are parents of these unpredictable individuals, can this information help us navigate those difficult years and assist our children in becoming more thoughtful, reflective, and empathetic adults? If we are teachers, how can this new knowledge and understanding help us become more effective teachers? What changes do we need to make in our teaching and classroom practices? If we are school administrators, what implications does it have for the ways we organize schools, develop and implement curricular and other educational programs, and generally facilitate effective teaching and learning in our schools? For staff and professional developers, how should it impact the services and learning opportunities we offer the teachers and other professionals with whom we work?

Figure 17.1 The Typical Teenage Brain?

For me, this new knowledge about the teenage brain and its development is both empowering and yet also somewhat daunting. It should fill us with great hope and high expectation. It shows us that adolescence offers perhaps a second chance—or at least an additional chance—to unleash the enormous potential and possibilities that lie within every person's brain and to shape positively that person's social, emotional, and intellectual development. It means that what happens to teenagers during their adolescent years is very important and can have a considerable and long-lasting impact on their lives. But it also presents a great challenge. This enhanced understanding of the development of the adolescent brain should make us realize that the things adults might do or not do can make tremendous differences in the lives of the teenagers with whom they work. This new knowledge can be particularly enlightening and hopeful for parents of troubled teens who may feel that all is lost and nothing can be done to change the course of future events. Despite that their kids may be engaging in highly disruptive and potentially dangerous behaviors, this new understanding of the teen brain suggests that this antisocial conduct might not be so firmly fixed and permanent. There is considerable hope for positive change and improvement given time and appropriate interventions. Knowing that the teenage brain is developing in some unexpected ways and undergoing tremendous change can help all of us see teenagers in a new light. Perhaps it will allow us to be more tolerant and forgiving of their transgressions, poor choices, and sometimes confusing and inexplicable behavior. It is both beneficial and of considerable comfort for both parents and teachers to understand, appreciate, and remember that the teenage brain is indeed a work in progress.

> Knowing that the teenage brain is developing in some unexpected ways and undergoing tremendous change can help all of us see teenagers in a new light.

A QUICK REVIEW: THE IMPORTANT THINGS WE HAVE LEARNED

It is useful for us to consider for a moment some of the important things we have learned about the teenage brain and its development. Among the most significant and relevant are the following:

• There is a dynamic period of brain growth and neural proliferation, consolidation, and refinement in the teen brain during adolescence.

• Much of the frustrating, conflicting, and often confusing behavior of teenagers has a biological basis and is due to the evolving and changing nature of the adolescent brain.

- The use-it-or-lose-it principle. The types and reliability of neural pathways developed in the teenage brain are largely determined by the diversity of activities and experiences in which the teen engages. Neural networks that get used and exercised are maintained and become more efficient. Those that are not get pruned away.

- The last part of the adolescent brain to fully mature is the prefrontal cortex—the area of the brain in which more rational, higher-level cognitive functioning takes place.

- Language and general communication skills become more complex and improve considerably during the teenage years.

- Teenagers process emotions differently than adults and often misread social situations and emotional signals from others.

- Teenagers often think with their amygdala—that is, their decision making is often based more in the emotional part of their brain than in the rational thinking part of the brain. Consequently, teenagers often have difficulty in seeing and appreciating the consequences of their actions and decisions.

- Teenagers are often motivationally impaired and frequently need concrete, short-term external motivation.

- Surges of sex hormones in the teen brain greatly influence the production of neurochemicals that affect and regulate mood and excitability in teenagers.

- Teens are more prone to impulsivity, risk taking, and reckless behavior because of chemical changes occurring within the pleasure-reward center of their brains.

- The teenage brain is particularly susceptible to stress and the possible long-term or permanent changes associated with substance use and abuse of all types.

- Many psychiatric and mental disorders first appear during the teenage years.

- Teens are more susceptible to addictions of all kinds. Teenage addictions are harder to overcome.

- Teens are often sleep deprived. Proper nutrition and quality rest is crucial for the developing teen brain.

- Physical activity is of great benefit to teenagers and their developing brains.

- Teenagers are highly social animals and greatly value peer relationships.

- Adolescence is a tumultuous and confusing time for teenagers (and their parents and teachers!) as they strive to gain autonomy, create a self-identity, and establish lasting personal relationships.

WHAT DO WE NEED TO DO TO HELP TEENAGERS REACH THEIR POTENTIAL?

There are many things that adults can do to help teenagers reach their fullest potential. Here are some great ideas to start with.

Parents

• Reassess and adjust your own perceptions about how adult teenagers are. Just because they are big and eat a lot does not mean that they are capable of thinking and behaving like adults.

• Try to maintain a positive and supportive atmosphere at home. Try to communicate regularly with your teens and talk to them about what bothers them and about their hopes, fears, and concerns. Listen!

• When assigning chores and household duties or discussing rules and responsibilities, be clear in stating your expectations and say what you mean.

• Avoid dominating or making all the difficult choices or decisions for your teenagers; instead, guide them through the tough ones. Help them see the possible consequences of their actions or decisions by suggesting or hinting at what might happen. Help teens understand the parameters of acceptable behavior and the possible consequences of ignoring such parameters.

• Expect and plan for possible attractions to risky behaviors. It is wiser to pay more attention and time assisting teens who get themselves in hot water than shaking our heads in disappointment or worse, ignoring the signs that our teens are engaging in such behaviors.

• Encourage (and try to model) regular physical activity and a healthy lifestyle (good nutrition, plenty of rest and relaxation, abstinence from drugs, appropriate relationships).

• Be aware of who your teen's friends are and what activities they share, but do not try to pick their friends or be critical of their choices.

• Provide your teen with some breathing room and privacy. Be understanding of their increasing need for personal and physical space.

• Establish clear and consistent limits and a structured environment for your teenagers, but try to do this through negotiation and by explaining the reasons for such limits. Allow teens to have some input into such things as rules and curfews. Teenagers need parents to be consistent and constant figures in their lives.

• Give your teenagers chances to make and learn from their mistakes and grow socially, emotionally, and intellectually. Making mistakes is really how the brain learns.

• Help teens achieve a healthy balance in their lives (social, sports, school, work, etc.). Try to prevent your teen from being overscheduled. Teens can be easily led to believe (by both parents and teachers) that the more activities they participate in, the better. Although it might look impressive on the teen's resume, it often comes at the price of chronic fatigue and sleep deprivation. The quality of commitment and performance always suffers.

• Help your teens with organizational strategies like calendars, daily planners, and goal setting. Help them establish appropriate daily schedules and nighttime routines that will provide for plenty of quality down time, rest, and sleep.

• Encourage your teens to participate in rich multifaceted activities like music, drama, or performing and visual arts—activities that have been shown to be more whole brain and that establish multiple neural pathways in the developing teenage brain. Try not to let your teenagers to become addicted to the more solitary sedentary activities like watching TV, playing video games, or surfing the Internet. Developing brains need challenging and socially engaging activities and experiences.

• Continue to stay involved with the school and informed about your teen's education and school activities.

• Try to avoid power struggles with your teenagers, particularly in situations where being right becomes the chief focus.

• Above all have a sense of humor! Show patience and empathy as your teens traverse this difficult period in their lives. Do not take things personally; remember teens are often thinking with their emotional brain and there are often biological reasons for their rebelliousness. Have faith that adolescent anxiety and emotional turmoil will pass.

Teachers

• Become knowledgeable about the teenage brain, how it is developing, and the implications for your classroom and teaching practice. Try to keep current on new research and scientific studies about the teenage brain, particularly those findings that clearly have some implications for teaching.

• Teach your teenage students about their developing brains and how this development is influencing their socioemotional and intellectual growth as well as their behavior and decision making. This knowledge can become quite empowering for teenagers.

• Help students assess and inventory their interests, strengths, and abilities; and use this information to make some well-informed decisions about which activities and experiences might be best for them.

• Encourage students to take on different challenges and experiences, but assist them in seeing that they will often learn more from several higher quality experiences and activities than numerous mediocre ones.

- Make certain that your teenage students are as developmentally ready as they need to be for the various learning experiences in which they are engaged. We need to be sure that they have the intellectual capacity and necessary context to understand the lessons that we might want them to learn.

- Recognize that older teens and younger teens are different and that they need different educational choices, degrees of freedom, and levels of challenge.

- Teachers often will need to be the external motivators for many adolescents—particularly younger teens. Explore and develop a repertoire of different ways of motivating teenagers and unlocking the intrinsic motivation that lies within each one.

- Provide a diverse and rich range of learning experiences that will stimulate many different neural networks in the teenage brain.

- Assist teenagers with organizational and goal-setting strategies and help them recognize what they need to do to achieve a level of balance in their lives.

- Experiment with and develop a diverse inventory of teaching and learning strategies and practices that prove to be particularly effective with adolescent students. Share these successful practices and techniques regularly with your professional colleagues.

- Make your own classroom brain compatible. Relish and enjoy the experience and challenge of working with these unpredictable people filled with such great potential. Know that what you do is extremely important and will have a lasting impact on their development. Research repeatedly shows us that the presence of a caring competent teacher is still the most important and significant factor in an effective classroom.

- Start using some of the ideas from this book tomorrow or on Monday morning!

Schools and School Administrators

- Create and support a culture of brain-compatible teaching and learning in your school. Make this a focus of your staff development and create a professional learning community in which teachers and other staff regularly and actively reflect upon and share their insights, knowledge, successes, and concerns about teaching adolescents.

- As the school educational leader, continue to stay as informed as possible about brain research and its impact on teaching and learning.

- Create a school that has a sense of community where all students feel safe, are valued, and are seen as learners and where parents or guardians feel welcomed as important partners in the education of their children.

- Create workshops and other learning opportunities for parents and other community members to learn about the teenage brain and brain-compatible teaching or learning.

- Create and support a middle level structure and school organization to help young adolescents make an easier and more successful transition to the high school model.

• Provide a mentoring and advisory program in your school.

• Provide a rich and varied range of educational programs in your school, including many opportunities for both curricular and cocurricular choices.

• Provide lots of opportunities for all students to be physically active during the school day. This should include activities that range from highly competitive interscholastic sports to more general participation fitness clubs. Offer both group and individual activities. Emphasis should be placed on physical activities that have carry-over potential into the community and adult life. Very few secondary students continue to play competitive sports beyond high school.

• Establish healthy eating programs in your school. Stress the importance of good nutrition and proper hydration for the developing teenage brain.

• Experiment with and try to organize school schedules and start and finish times that are more reflective of the teen brain's natural learning and sleep and awake cycles.

• Create a homework policy for your school that is more consistent with the needs of teenagers' down time and quality sleep. Three or four hours of school-assigned work every night is undoubtedly unreasonable, unrealistic, and bound to be a source of conflict.

• Make multidisciplinary, interdisciplinary, or cross-curricular studies an integral part of your school's educational programming.

• Provide opportunities for adolescent students to engage in more real-world educational experiences like internships, mentoring, apprenticeship, and community and service learning.

• Seriously consider organizing school schedules and graduation requirements so that students might take a year off for such things as work, apprenticeship, travel, or charitable service.

Staff and Professional Developers

• Become well informed (and keep up to date) about brain research and its implications for schools and teaching practice.

• Provide teachers and other professionals with many opportunities to learn about and help them to obtain current, timely, and concise information on brain-compatible teaching.

• Model brain-compatible teaching or learning in your own workshops, seminars, and other professional development opportunities that you facilitate.

• Help plan and facilitate workshops about the brain and brain-compatible teaching or learning for parents and other community members.

SOME FINAL THOUGHTS:
OPENING DOORWAYS TO POSSIBILITIES

In the final analysis, what is the ultimate promise of our enhanced understanding of the teenage brain and how it develops? The promise lies in our recognition that there are great doorways to possibilities opening in the teenage brain during this critical time of development—doorways to more highly refined and productive social and emotional skills; doorways for the development and acquisition of languages, for increased facility in and appreciation of music and artistic expression, for the development and refinement of physical skills and athletic abilities; and doorways for the development of advanced cognitive abilities in reasoning, decision making, reflection, and problem solving. These doorways exist because of the general plasticity of the teenage brain and the tremendous proliferation and pruning of neural pathways occurring during adolescence. But these doorways are open for only a relatively short period of time. Without frequent and proper use, these doorways to such immense possibilities can close quickly and disappear altogether. It means that all of us who work with teenagers need to provide many diverse and varied experiences and learning opportunities that will enable them to open up and sustain as many of these doorways to possibilities as they can.

> There are great doorways to possibilities opening in the teenage brain during this critical time of development.

Perhaps the most positive and significant idea to come from this increased understanding of the brain is the recognition that thinking can be taught—thinking in its many forms and the myriad of ways of looking at and understanding the world. And here is the really exciting part—it means that sound, effective teaching is even more critical and important than we ever imagined! Sound, effective teaching will help to reveal and open these many doorways to possibilities in the adolescent mind. Quality teaching will assist teenagers to lubricate the hinges of their many doorways and keep these open so that important neural pathways for learning and memory can be established, strengthened, and sustained. In this way we can ensure that the great potential of these teenage minds can be unleashed and developed to the fullest.

This we do know. If we attend to those things that we recognize the brain needs for optimal learning, then **all** our students will have greater opportunities to become successful and effective learners. In the end, that is what all parents and teachers want.

WANTED: AN EPIDEMIC FOR AN IDEA

Malcolm Gladwell (2000), in his bestseller book *The Tipping Point: How Little Things Can Make a Big Difference*, presents the thesis that an idea, a fashion trend, a fad, a new product, or type of social behavior often reaches a certain point or threshold (the "tipping point") when it suddenly begins to spread like an epidemic. He suggests that such things as innovations and trends often spread in the same ways that viruses can cause an infectious disease contagion. The most intriguing component of Gladwell's hypothesis is the premise that such epidemics of ideas (e.g., brain-compatible teaching) occur because of the influence of only a relatively few people (people Gladwell calls "connectors") coupled with the essential truthfulness or attractiveness of the idea. What is most critical in causing this spread of an idea is that the people committed to the idea translate it for their wider circle of friends and associates into a more useful and useable form. Translation means communicating the idea in easy to understand and plain language complemented with practical and workable examples of how to apply or take advantage of this new idea in their own particular situations. I hope that I have been able to serve as a translator, but we really need every teacher to become a connector and translator to help spread the epidemic of this new science of learning—that is, brain-compatible teaching—throughout his or her school, circle of friends, professional colleagues, and school district. Do not wait. Creating the brain-compatible classroom or school is not a simple or quick undertaking. But all important destinations are reached by taking a first step. Take that important first step in your next class, tomorrow morning, or on Monday. Discover the ways to unleash the potential that lies in the brains of all your teenage students. Spread the contagion of these exciting new ideas among your friends and colleagues.

Glossary

Academic Prompt (Wiggins & McTighe, 1998)—open-ended questions or problems that cannot be answered by just recalling information or facts studied in class. Students are required to critically analyze and evaluate the question and prepare some type of response to summarize their understanding.

Activators and Advance Organizers—short learning activities or exercises that are used to introduce a class, topic, or new subject. Activating prior knowledge is key to effective teaching and learning. Many of the other strategies listed—for example, word splash, where I stand, right on target, and idea map—can be used as activators.

Active Listening—an interpersonal communication strategy where students are taught to listen carefully to what another student is expressing, to paraphrase it, to ask for clarification, to restate and reflect upon it, and finally to validate the other's feelings, viewpoints, or opinions. An integral part of successful mediation and conflict resolution techniques.

Affirmations—positive statements, actions, rituals, or procedures that are intended to affirm and encourage student involvement, positive behaviors, and achievement of learning goals.

Alphabet Soup (Saphier & Haley, 1993)—a review strategy or advance organizer in which students draw a letter from a container or are assigned one by the teacher and create a response beginning with that letter that summarizes some aspect of the topic or subject being studied.

Analogy Chart—a chart in which students compare a familiar known event, item, or concept to another seemingly unrelated one to provide clarification about the second idea. Often uses several prompts or questions to which students respond to both ideas. For example, one might chart how conducting a criminal trial is like writing an effective persuasive essay: Who do you need to convince? What evidence will you use? How will you present it? How will you summarize?

Anticipation Guide (Buehl, 2001; Herber, 1978)—a series of statements to which students respond (usually agree or disagree) prior to reading content material. Intended to activate students' ideas, opinions, and viewpoints about the major concepts contained within the reading.

130

Authentic Assessment—assessments that generally ask students to demonstrate what they know and can do by creating, producing, performing, or doing something else that can be applied to situations or problems that have a more real-world context. Examples include individual or group projects, portfolios, journals, investigative reports, and performance assessments.

"Can Do" Language—teacher talk and language that conveys ideas of success and achievement for students, for example, a teacher might say, "I know all of you will be able to do this."

Carousel Brainstorming—a brainstorming and idea-generating strategy in which groups of students move about the classroom responding to questions or prompts written on chart paper. Can also be accomplished by rotating charts around classroom from one student group to another.

Case Studies—generalized stories or descriptions of an actual or fictional event, situation, or circumstance requiring students to analyze and evaluate the problem or issue and propose solutions.

ChecBric (Lewin & Shoemaker, 1998)—an assessment tool that combines features of a checklist and a rubric. It usually indicates the absence or presence of a particular skill or trait (checklist) and also provides some measure of quality of the skill (rubric).

Circle of Friends—a conflict resolution and mediation strategy in which students share their feelings, frustrations, or concerns with a group of peers sitting in a circle arrangement. Friends collectively attempt to validate the feelings, to mediate solutions, and to offer advice.

Concept Attainment and Concept Formation—inductive teaching strategies in which the teacher provides information or sets of data in which students look for common characteristics or patterns to identify the central idea or concept.

Concept Circles—a paper (card stock) circle is divided into four or more equal segments on which are written words or phrases all related to a bigger idea or concept. The individual segments are cut out and mixed with equal sized segments from other similar concepts. Student groups must sort out all the segments that relate to the central concepts and reconstruct the original large concept circles. Can also be used by requiring students to create concept segments when teacher gives the main concept or by filling in only two or three segments and requiring students to add additional ones.

Concept Map—a graphic organizer in which students map out the related ideas or subtopics of a central concept or idea. General format includes interrelated ideas (words or phrases) linked by connecting pathways identified with brief explanatory note or phrase.

Contract Learning—an assessment strategy in which student and teacher mutually agree (i.e., contract) on a series of assignments, activities, and learning experiences that the student must complete to satisfy the evaluation requirements for a particular unit of study. Students frequently select from a range of opportunities suggested by the teacher and can suggest their own choices as well.

Cooperative Learning—a term used to describe any learning activities where groups of students work together collaboratively and cooperatively in order to complete the task or activity. Activities are structured so that all members contribute and are dependent on one another for mutual success.

Decision Grid and Decision Tree—a graphic organizer where students can identify a central problem and use the branches to illustrate all the possible courses of action and reasons for particular decisions.

Descriptive Feedback—oral and written information given to students about their progress in achieving certain learning outcomes. Provides clear information about what they have achieved successfully and offers suggestions about what they should try or need to do to reach their learning objectives.

Door Pass—a quick review and reflection strategy at the end of a class or beginning of next class. Students must answer questions, respond to a prompt, or supply some information about class on an index card and give to teacher as permission to leave or enter.

Dramatizations—in dramatizations, groups of students summarize and represent their understandings about a particular subject, topic, or idea using the medium of drama. Students decide upon the best way to represent their knowledge, create and script a scene or short play, and then perform it for their class or other audience.

Elaborative Rehearsal Strategies—a wide variety of learning strategies that are designed to help the learner apply, review, analyze, or elaborate on the information in such ways as to increase understanding and retention of the information.

Energizers and Energy Breaks—short (two to five minutes) physical activities designed to increase energy levels in the brain or to provide a change in attention or focus levels. These generally are designed to energize and stimulate both the body and brain of students.

Essential Questions (Wiggins & McTighe, 1998)—questions that go to the heart of a central idea or problem and raise other related issues or questions. Used as an organizing frame for inquiry into topic or subject and to help students identify relationships and connections.

Fact Cards—a review or rehearsal strategy in which cards containing different facts or pieces of information about the topic just studied are distributed among members of the cooperative group. The group must complete some assignment that uses the information from the fact cards. The assignment is completed collaboratively as all members search their own fact cards to determine if the necessary information can be found on their individual cards.

Facts and Fibs—a review or rehearsal strategy in which students create on an index card several statements that are true (facts) for the topic or subject just studied and one statement that is false (fib). Students pair up or form small groups with other students, and then other students must determine which statement is the fib and give reasons for their choices.

Four Corners—in this strategy, teachers pose a question and provide four possible answers or responses—each one posted in one of four corners of the room. Students are asked to stand in the corner that best corresponds to the answer they believe to be correct or best aligns with their viewpoint.

Four Square Summary—a graphic organizer where a page is divided into four equal squares. Students must compile a summary of a topic by responding to the prompts in each square. Usually includes both written and graphic responses.

Gallery Walk—a cooperative learning strategy where student groups move (in a specific time frame, e.g., two minutes at each stop) around classroom looking at the posted work of other student groups. This usually follows an activity where student groups have had to complete a summary of their work on chart paper.

Graphic Organizers—a wide variety of graphical formats that enable students to represent, organize, categorize, summarize, and reflect upon their knowledge and understanding of particular topics, ideas, or concepts.

Group Investigators—a more structured cooperative learning approach in which students identify an inquiry question or problem, develop a plan of action for investigating the question, then collect and compile research, and present a report on the question to the class or some other audience.

Guided Visualization—a strategy in which the teacher asks students to visualize mentally a particular event, situation, or scenario while he or she reads a script describing the event. This is usually followed by the students writing, drawing, or otherwise describing their reactions, feelings, or ideas.

Idea Map—a graphic organizer that asks students to generate as many subsidiary or connected ideas as possible around a central idea or concept.

Inside and Outside Circle (Kagan, 1994)—a cooperative learning structure in which one group of students forms a group inside another group with the inside group facing outward and outside group facing inward. Face to face partners review ideas, answer questions, or complete a brief task in a short period of time (e.g., one or two minutes).

Jigsawing (Aronson et al., 1978)—a highly structured cooperative learning activity where students begin in home groups, separate into expert groups, complete a learning task, then return to home groups where student experts teach other members of home group.

Key Word or Phrase—in this strategy the teacher provides a key word or phrase for a given topic, idea, or concept and students must generate related ideas for each of the letters in the key word or phrase.

Kinesthetic Flow Charts and Diagrams—a strategy where the teacher maps out on the floor any idea or concept that can be summarized in a cycle, sequence, or regular order. Students move through the diagram following a script of the steps or stages of the concept.

Know Books (Abernathy & Reardon, 2003)—a student generated and created textbook or portfolio containing a collection of notes, drawings, sketches, pictures, or other graphics along with handwritten, typed, or computer-generated notes that represent the current level of knowledge and understanding the student has about a particular topic, subject, or unit of study. Excellent assessment tool.

KWL (Ogle, 1986)—a graphic organizer often used to preview a new topic of study and to summarize the new knowledge. Normally a three-column chart (Know, Want to know, Learned) that students complete prior to, during, and after the learning experience.

Learning Centers—a teaching and learning strategy in which students complete a series of learning tasks or activities at a number of assigned stations or centers. Typically students rotate (over a period of several days or more) through a series of stations that all have activities or learning experiences related to a central topic or concept.

Learning Logs—a student journal in which the student identifies learning goals and objectives and records the progress towards achieving those goals. Often includes prompts provided by teachers requiring students to reflect upon the learning process and to identify the next steps.

Learning Partners—a cooperative learning strategy where students are paired as learning partners and, at certain times throughout class or day, must share their learning, reflect upon their understanding, or complete a task together.

Learning Style Inventories—a wide range of assessment tools and rating scales, which students can use to identify and evaluate their particular learning styles

Looping (Bulla, 2000)—a review strategy in which students compile review questions and answers (note: the answer to a particular question is always on a different card) on cards about a topic or concept. Each student is then given one Q and A card; and using this set of Q and A cards, the class then reviews the topic by asking and answering each question orally one by one in sequence. The looping review continues until all questions and answers have been given and the loop ends up back at the first student to have asked a question.

Metaphors—a powerful way for students to demonstrate their understanding of a particular idea, topic, or concept. It involves identifying a general pattern in a specific topic or concept and then finding the same pattern in another idea or concept that seemingly is quite different.

Mind Maps—a graphic organizer in which students map out their understanding of an idea or topic by creating a written and drawn map of the idea by combining words, short phrases, symbols, sketches, or caricatures that provide a very personal summary of the idea or topic. Often mind maps feature the use of colors to help clarify the relationships and interconnectedness of the contributing factors.

Mnemonics and Memory Aids—an elaborative rehearsal strategy that uses key words, acrostic sentences, acronyms, pegging rhymes, physical cues, or any number of other memory devices to help students review and remember semantic information.

Multiple Intelligence Inventories and Assessments—an inventory of attributes, characteristics, or behaviors that are typically associated with various multiple intelligences and that can help students identify and classify their own particular multiple intelligences.

Music—music should be used in a wide variety of ways in the brain-compatible classroom: providing background music during activities, establishing mood and mind state, signaling beginning and ending of lesson phases, teaching specific content, and creating memory aids by reinforcing concepts and assessments (e.g., students create their own piggyback songs).

Numbered Heads (Kagan, 1994)—a cooperative learning strategy in which the students in a particular group are all numbered so that the teacher may call upon a single person in the group at any time to represent the understanding of the group. For example, "I want student #3 to answer this question for the group."

Observation Checklists—data or tracking sheets that identify certain skills and abilities and that allow teachers to observe, document, and provide feedback to students about the acquisition of these skills and abilities.

One Best Way to Remember—a review strategy in which students are to create a phrase or invented word or phrase to remember (i.e., recall later) an important concept, idea, or topic. For example, *convecorofront*—an invented word to remind students of the three main ways in which precipitation forms—convectional, orographic, frontal.

One-Minute Commercial—an excellent way for student groups to demonstrate their understanding of a particular idea, concept, or topic. Students are given a short period of time to create a one-minute commercial and then perform for the class to summarize what they understand about the topic just studied.

One-Minute Reviews—a strategy in which students turn to or find their learning partners and then within one-minute each reviews quickly what they know and understand about the topic being studied.

One-Word Journal (Angelo & Cross, 1993)—a strategy in which students review information just learned or read and attempt to summarize it in a single word in their journal. Students must not only identify a suitable word, but they must also explain why this particular word so succinctly and effectively summarizes the main idea.

PBL (Problem-Based Learning)—a learning strategy in which students work in groups to solve a more real-world problem or question. Students research the problem, prioritize the information, develop possible courses of action, and then produce a final product or solution for the initial problem. A strategy in which students apply their understanding rather than just restate what the teacher has taught them.

Peer Mediation—a conflict resolution strategy in which specially trained students help other students resolve disagreements by mediating their discussion and analysis of the problem.

Personal Growth Portfolio—an authentic assessment format in which students document their personal growth and learning for a particular unit of study by compiling a collection of work samples together with their reflections on what and how they have learned from these samples.

Physical Modeling—a kinesthetic teaching strategy in which students physically demonstrate or role-play their understanding of a concept or idea, for example, movement of planets in solar system.

Picture This—a teaching strategy in which students analyze a provocative, intriguing, or otherwise interesting photograph using question prompts provided by the teacher.

For example, a teacher might say, "What do you think has happened in this picture?"

Piggyback Song—a song in which the lyrics are rewritten to teach some idea or concept, but the song uses the tune and melody of another very familiar song.

Placemat Response—a group brainstorming strategy in which a large sheet of paper (i.e., the placemat) is placed on a table so that all three or four members of a group can at the same time write their ideas or responses about a certain question or prompt posed by the teacher.

PMI (de Bono, 1986)—Plus, Minus, Interesting: a graphic organizer in which students reflect upon what they have learned by identifying the most positive or important aspect of an issue, the negative or unclear component, and finally something interesting or requiring further study.

Q & A Match—a teaching strategy in which one half of the students in the class receive question cards and the other half, answer cards. The strategy requires students to move around the class, discuss the topic with classmates, and find the best match between Q (question) and A (answer) cards. A good way to introduce a new topic, but it can also be used very effectively as a review or an assessment method.

Quick Draws—on a prompt from the teacher, each student quickly sketches what comes to mind about the idea or subject. For example, a prompt might ask, "What comes to mind when you think of the word *conflict?*"

Reciprocal Teaching—a cooperative learning strategy in which learning partners take turns clarifying, summarizing, and teaching each other new subject matter. Often used with a required reading selection from a text.

Reflection Journals—an assessment strategy in which students are asked to write and reflect about their own learning using prompts provided by the teacher.

Reflective Questioning—questions that ask students to reflect upon, summarize, synthesize, and analyze their learning rather than just regurgitate information from teacher.

Right on Target—a quick assessment strategy in which students indicate how much they know or have learned about a topic by indicating how close they are to the center of a circular target. (Center of target being highest level of knowledge.)

Role Playing—one form of dramatization in which students assume the role of a particular person (fictional or historical) to demonstrate their level of understanding about a particular idea, topic, or concept, for example, a certain officer during a particular Civil War battle.

Roving Investigators—a strategy in which certain students move about (i.e., rove) the classroom trying to find out from other students as much as they can about a certain topic or subject of study. Often class is divided into two groups—those who are investigators and those who have the information.

Sequence Cards (Pictures)—a series of cards that document steps, stages, or phases of a particular event, concept, or idea, for example, stages of cell mitosis or events preceding the American Revolution. Students must arrange cards physically in the correct order and be prepared to explain and defend their decisions.

Service Learning—a form of community based education in which students perform some project or service in the community that can also be related to learning outcomes in school, for example, a river restoration project as part of a high school biology course.

Simulations—learning activities that are modeled after or try to simulate real-world situations. For example, students in an economics class might create a stimulated business of a particular type and role-play the various stake holders and situations that might involve a business of that type in the real world.

Six Thinking Hats (de Bono, 1985)—a critical thinking strategy that requires students to examine an issue or problem from six different perspectives (i.e., put on six different thinking hats).

Slow Reveal—an introductory or review strategy where the teacher slowly (piece by piece) reveals a picture, image, or some sort of puzzle related to a topic about to be studied or that has already been studied. Each reveal is usually accompanied by some verbal clue as well. Students must try to identify the image or concept using the fewest clues and reveals.

Sort Cards and Pictures—a series of cards or pictures that can be grouped or categorized into various categories of classifications (e.g., types of animals that might be classified into backbones or no backbones, land or water, mammals or reptiles, etc.). Students are given the cards to physically sort into categories and to explain their classification schemes.

Student Start-Ups—a teaching strategy in which students are given the responsibility for researching a new topic to be studied and to design and develop some creative way of introducing the topic to the rest of the class.

Tableaux—a form of dramatization in which groups research and create a single frozen picture as a way of summarizing some situation, event, or concept that they have studied.

Team-Games-Tournament—Similar to jigsawing but usually used as a review or check of understanding. Students begin in home groups of three or four and review information previously learned then break into tournament groups composed of one member from three or four other home groups. Tournament group members are tested using questions usually written on game cards and keep records of each member's performance. After each tournament group completes a rotation of a certain number of questions or answers as many questions as possible in a certain time frame, each member then returns to the home base group and the score from each individual student is used to tabulate a cumulative score for the home group.

Thermometer of Learning—a quick assessment of student learning or level of understanding. Students mark or indicate on a large thermometer where they believe their level of knowledge falls. The thermometer ranges from "really cool" (I know very little about this) at the bottom of the thermometer to "very hot" (I could teach this) at the top of the thermometer.

Think-Pair-Share (Kagan, 1994)—a cooperative learning structure in which pairs of students first individually think about a question or prompt from the teacher and then pair up to share their ideas or thinking on the topic.

Trash Your Troubles—an anger management or cooling-down strategy where students write what is bothering them on a piece of paper, ball it up, and then trash their troubles in the garbage can.

Unravel This—A good elaborative rehearsal strategy where student groups are given a number of index cards on which are written various terms or ideas related to a central concept. Students also receive a number of pieces of string or yarn on which are attached cards describing some action phrase or verb. The challenge is for the students to link all the cards and pieces of string to show relationships and interconnectedness between and among all the items (i.e., to create a physical concept map or web of a central concept).

Vocabulary Sort and Predict (adapted from Nova Scotia Department of Education, 1999)—This strategy is a good one to use to introduce or review all the important vocabulary words prior to beginning a new unit of study. Teacher lists 10 to 20 key words from the unit of study, and student groups are asked to categorize and sort words into three or four categories with a specific name or title for each category. Particularly effective when students can actually cut out the words from a paper list and physically arrange the words into categories on a master sheet.

Where I Stand—a quick standing survey of students' opinions on a question or controversial statement posed by teacher. Students arrange themselves along an imaginary line from one side of the classroom to the other where one side represents "strongly agree" to the other side which represents "strongly disagree."

Word Splash—an activating activity designed to get students thinking about what they may already know about a topic or subject or to speculate about the possible connections among groups of words or terms associated with the new topic of study. The words are arranged randomly (i.e., splashed) on a page and projected for students to see.

Workshop—a teaching and learning strategy in which students focus on the development and improvement of particular skills while completing a major activity or work assignment combined with frequent coaching and feedback from the teacher on the particular skills. For example, while working on a study of local history, students are given assistance and ongoing coaching in the development of historical research and documentation skills.

Write It and Draw It—a journaling technique where students are asked to both describe verbally (i.e., write it) and sketch (i.e., draw it) their understanding and knowledge about a particular topic, idea, or concept. Typically the journal page is divided into two columns for the writing component and the drawing one.

Zeros and X's (Hughes & Vass, 2001)—This strategy uses the traditional tic-tac-toe grid of nine numbered squares on which students will record answers. The teacher asks nine questions matched to the nine squares. Students receive a zero for a correct answer and an X for an incorrect one. The objective for this review game is to record three zeros in a row—vertically, horizontally, or diagonally. The teacher attempts to arrange questions so that all students can enjoy success at some point.

Suggested Readings

Abernathy, R., & Reardon, M. (2003). *Hot tips for teachers: 30+ steps to student engagement.* Tucson, AZ: Zephyr Press.

Beecher, M. (1995). *Developing the gifts and talents of all students in the regular classroom.* Mansfield Center, CT: Creative Learning Press.

Bellanca, J. (1990). *The cooperative think tank: Graphic organizers to teach thinking in the cooperative classroom.* Thousand Oaks, CA: Corwin Press.

Bellanca, J. (1992). *The cooperative think tank II: Graphic organizers to teach thinking in the cooperative classroom.* Thousand Oaks, CA: Corwin Press.

Bennett, B., & Rolheiser, C. (2001). *Beyond Monet: The artful science of instructional integration.* Toronto, Canada: Bookation.

Buehl, D. (2001). *Classroom strategies for interactive learning.* Newark, DE: International Reading Association.

Campbell, L. (2003). *Mindful learning: 101 proven strategies for student and teacher success.* Thousand Oaks, CA: Corwin Press.

Guillaume, A., Yopp, R., & Yopp, H. (2007). *50 strategies for active teaching.* Prentice Hall, NJ: Pearson Merrill.

Herrell, A., & Jordan, M. (2007). *35 management strategies.* Prentice Hall, NJ: Pearson Merrill.

Hughes, M., & Vass, A. (2001). *Strategies for closing the learning gap.* Stafford, Great Britain: Network Educational Press Ltd.

Jensen, E. (1998a). *Introduction to brain-compatible learning.* Thousand Oaks, CA: Corwin Press.

Jensen, E. (1998b). *Super teaching.* Thousand Oaks, CA: Corwin Press.

Kagan, S., & Kagan, M. (1998). *Multiple intelligences: The complete MI book.* San Clemente, CA: Kagan Cooperative Learning.

Lipton, L., & Wellman, B. (1999). *Pathways to understanding: Patterns and practice in the learning-focused classroom* (2nd ed.). Guilford, VA: Pathways Publishing.

Marzano, R., Pickering, D., & Pollock, J. (2001). *Classroom instruction that works: Research-based strategies for increasing student achievement.* Alexandria, VA: Association for Supervision and Curriculum Development.

Obenchain, K., & Morris, R. (2007). *50 social studies strategies for K—8 classrooms* (2nd ed.). Prentice Hall, NJ: Pearson Merrill.

Rogers, S., & Graham, S. (1997). *The high performance toolbox.* Evergreen, CO: Peak Learning System.

Rogers, S., Ludington, J., & Graham, S. (1998). *Motivation and learning.* Evergreen, CO: Peak Learning Systems.

Saphier, J., & Haley, M. (1993a). *Activators: Activity structures to engage students' thinking before instruction.* Carlisle, MA: Research for Better Teaching.

Saphier, J. & Haley, M. (1993b). *Summarizers: Activity structures to support integration and retention of new learning.* Carlisle, MA: Research for Better Teaching.

Silberman, M. (1996). *Active learning: 101 strategies to teach any subject*. Boston: Allyn & Bacon.

Smokler, D. (2005). *Making learning come alive*. Thousand Oaks, CA: Corwin Press.

Tate, M. (2003). *Worksheets don't grow dendrites*. Thousand Oaks, CA: Corwin Press.

Wiggins, G., & McTighe, J. (1998). *Understanding by design*. Alexandria, VA: Association for Supervision and Curriculum Development.

Wood, K. (1994). *Practical strategies for improving instruction*. Columbus, OH: National Middle School Association.

Zemelman, S., Daniels, H., & Hyde, A. (1998). *Best practice: New standards for teaching and learning in America's schools* (2nd ed.). Portsmouth, NH: Heinemann Publishing.

Bibliography

Abernathy, R., & Reardon, M. (2003). *Hot tips for teachers: 30+ steps to student engagement*. Tucson, AZ: Zephyr Press.

American Academy of Child and Adolescent Psychiatry. (2001, June). Normal adolescent development part I. *Facts for Families* (No. 57). Retrieved September 27, 2005, from www.aacap.org/publications/factsfam/develop.htm

American Academy of Neurology. (2004, April 28). Language 'center' of brain shifts with age. *ScienceDaily*. Retrieved March 14, 2007, from http://www.sciencedaily.com/releases/2004/04/040428062634.htm (Adapted from a news release issued by American Academy of Neurology)

Angelo, T. A., & Cross, K. P. (1993). *Classroom assessment techniques: A handbook for college teachers* (2nd ed.). San Francisco, CA: Jossey Bass.

Armstrong, T. (2000). *Multiple intelligences in the classroom* (2nd. ed.). Alexandria, VA: Association for Supervision and Curriculum Development.

Aronson, E., Blaney, N., Stephin, C., Sikes, J., & Snapp, M. (1978). *The jigsaw classroom*. Thousand Oaks, CA: Sage Publications.

Ball, Sir Christopher. (2001, February). *OECD report on second high forum on brain mechanisms and youth learning*. Granada, Spain: Organisation for Economic Co-operation and Development.

Begley, S. (2000, February 28). Getting inside a teen brain. *Newsweek, 135*(9), 58-69.

Bennett, B., & Rolheiser, C. (2001). *Beyond Monet: The artful science of instructional integration*. Toronto, Ontario: Bookation.

Bransford, J., Brown, A., & Cocking, R. (Eds). (2000). *How people learn: Brain, mind, experience, and school* (Expanded ed.). Washington, DC: National Academy Press.

Briggs, K. C., & Myers, I. B. (1977). *Myers-Briggs type indicator*. Palo Alto, CA: Consulting Psychologists Press.

Brooks, J., & Brooks, M. (1993). *The case for constructivist classrooms*. Alexandria, VA: Association for Supervision and Curriculum Development.

Bruner, J. (1966). *Toward a theory of instruction*. Cambridge, MA: Harvard University Press.

Bruner, J. S., Goodnow, J. J., & Austin, G. A. (1986). *A study of thinking*. New Brunswick, NJ: Transaction Press.

Buehl, D. (2001). *Classroom strategies for interactive learning*. Newark, DE: International Reading Association.

Bulla, D. (2000), *Loops for learning: Memory boosters across the curriculum*. Tucson, AZ: Zephyr Press.

Caine, R., & Caine, G. (1994). *Making connections: Teaching and the human brain*. Reading, MA: Addison-Wesley Publishing.

Caine, R., & Caine, G. (1997). *Education on the edge of possibility*. Alexandria, VA: Association for Supervision and Curriculum Development.

Costa, A. (1995). *Teaching for intelligent behavior: Outstanding strategies for strengthening your students' thinking skills.* Bellevue, WA: Bureau of Education and Research.

Daniels, H., Bizar, M., & Zemelman, S. (2001). *Rethinking high school.* Portsmouth, NH: Heinemann Press.

Davis, A. (2000). *Making classroom assessment work.* Courtenay, BC, Canada: Connections Publishing.

Davis, J. (2004, April 15). Math heads: How do they do it? *WebMD.* Retrieved October 17, 2005, from http://my.webmd.com/content/Article/85/98705.htm

de Bono, E. (1985). *Six thinking hats.* Toronto, Ontario: Little, Brown & Company.

de Bono, E. (1986). *CoRT Thinking.* Toronto, Ontario: Little, Brown and Company.

de Bono, E. (1992). *Serious creativity: Using the power of lateral thinking to create new ideas.* New York: Harper Business.

Delisle, R. (1997). *How to use problem-based learning in the classroom.* Alexandria, VA: Association for Supervision and Curriculum Development.

DeVries, D., & Edwards, K. (1973). Learning games and student teams: Their effect on classroom process. *American Research Journal, 10,* 307-318.

Dunn, R., & Dunn, K. (1993). *Teaching secondary students through their individual learning styles.* Boston: Allyn & Bacon.

Ekwall, E. & Shanker, J. L. (1988). *Diagnosis and remediation of the disabled reader, 3rd Ed.* Boston, MA: Allyn & Bacon.

Erlauer, L. (2003). *The brain-compatible classroom: Using what we know about learning to improve teaching.* Alexandria, VA: Association for Supervision and Curriculum Development.

Ernest, P. (1995). The one and the many. In L. Steffe & J. Gale (Eds.), *Constructivism in education,* 459–486. Hillsdale, NJ: Lawrence Erlbaum.

Fanning, D. (Executive Producer). (2002, January 31) *Frontline: Inside the teenage brain* [Television broadcast]. Boston: Public Broadcasting Service. Retrieved September 21, 2005, from http://www.pbs.org/wgbh/pages/frontline/shows/teenbrain/

Feuerstein, R. (1980). *Instrumental enrichment: An intervention program for cognitive modifiability.* Glenview, IL: Scott Foresman and Company.

Fick, S., & Shilts, E. (2006, January/February). This is your brain on music. *Canadian Geographic, 126,* 34-35.

Frieden, J. (2000, August 21). Teen sleep deprivation a serious problem. *WebMD.* Retrieved October 10, 2005, from http://my.webmd.com/content/Article/27/1728_60579.htm

Fogarty, R. (1997). *Brain-compatible classrooms.* Thousand Oaks, CA: Corwin Press.

Fogarty, R. (1998). Intelligence-friendly classrooms: It just makes sense. *Phi Delta Kappan, 79*(9), 655-657.

Gabriel, J. (2001, June). More than just physical: PE and cognitive performance. *BrainConnection.com.* Retrieved April 25, 2004, from www.brainconnection.com/content/13_1

Gardner, H. (1983). *Frames of mind: The theory of multiple intelligences.* New York: Bantam Books.

Gillis, J. (2005, December 28). Anti-drug program in schools questioned. *The Chronicle Herald,* p. B2.

Gladwell, M. (2000). *The tipping point: How little things can make a big difference.* New York: Little, Brown & Company.

Goleman, D. (1995). *Emotional intelligence: Why it can matter more than IQ.* New York: Bantam Books.

Gregorc, A. (1979). Learning/teaching styles: Their nature and effects. In *Student learning styles: diagnosing and prescribing programs* (pp. 19-26). Reston, VA: National Association of Secondary School Principals.

Guillaume, A., Yopp, R., & Yopp, H. (2007). *50 strategies for active teaching*. Prentice Hall, NJ: Pearson Merrill.

Hanson, J. R., & Silver, H. F. (1998). *Learning styles and strategies: Who am I as a learner? teacher? what are my assets? liabilities? how can I work more effectively with students? teachers? parents? administrators?* Woodbridge, NJ: Thoughtful Education Press.

Hart, L. (1998). *Human brain and human learning*. Kent, WA: Books for Educators.

Healy, J. (1994). *Your child's growing mind*. New York: Bantam Doubleday Books.

Herber, H. (1978). *Teaching reading in content areas* (2nd ed.). Englewood Cliffs, NJ: Prentice-Hall.

Huebner, A. (2000). *Adolescent growth and development* (Publication No. 350-850). Retrieved September 27, 2005, from Virginia State University, Virginia Cooperative Extension Web site: http://www.ext.vt.edu/pubs/family/350-850/350-850.html

Hughes, M. (1999). *Closing the learning gap*. Stafford, Great Britain: Network Educational Press Ltd.

Hughes, M., & Vass, A. (2001). *Strategies for closing the learning gap*. Stafford, Great Britain: Network Educational Press Ltd.

Jensen, E. (1995). *The learning brain*. San Diego, CA: The Brain Store.

Jensen, E. (1996). *Completing the puzzle: The brain-compatible approach to learning*. Thousand Oaks, CA: Corwin Press.

Jensen, E. (1998a). *Introduction to brain-compatible learning*. Thousand Oaks, CA: Corwin Press.

Jensen, E. (1998b). *Super teaching*. Thousand Oaks, CA: Corwin Press.

Jensen, E. (1998c). *Teaching with the brain in mind*. Alexandria, VA: Association for Supervision and Curriculum Development.

Jensen, E. & Dabney, M. (2000). *Learning smarter: The new science of teaching*. Thousand Oaks, CA: Corwin Press.

Jonassen, D. (1991). Evaluating constructivist learning. *Educational Technology, 36*(9), 28-33.

Jonassen, D. (1994). Thinking technology. *Educational Technology, 34*(4), 34-37.

Kagan, S. (1994). *Cooperative learning*. San Clemente, CA: Kagan Cooperative Learning.

Kaufeldt, M. (1999). *Begin with the brain: Orchestrating the learner-centered classroom*. Tucson, AZ: Zephyr Press.

Kotulak, R. (2004, March). Exercise for the body is food for brain, study says. *Brain in the News, 11*(3), 7. (Reprinted from *The Chicago Tribune*, p. C1, 2004, March 17)

Kovalik, S. (1994). ITI, *the model: Integrated thematic instruction*. Kent, WA: Books for Educators.

Lewin, L., & Shoemaker, B. J. (1998). *Great performances: Creating classroom-based assessment task*. Alexandria, VA: Association for Supervision and Curriculum Development

Marzano, R. (1998). *A theory-based meta-analysis of research on instruction*. Aurora, CO: Mid-continent Research for Education and Learning.

Marzano, R., Pickering, D., & Pollock, J. (2001). *Classroom instruction that works: Research-based strategies for increasing student achievement*. Alexandria, VA: Association for Supervision and Curriculum Development.

McCarthy, B. (1980). *The 4MAT system: Teaching to learning styles with right or left mode techniques*. Barrington, IL: Excel.

McPhee, D. (1996). *Limitless learning: Making powerful learning an everyday event*. Tucson, AZ: Zephyr Press.

MedlinePlus. (2007, February 14). Adolescent development. Retrieved March 21, 2007, from http://www.nlm.nih.gov/medlineplus/ency/article/002003.htm

National Institute of Mental Health. (2001). Teenage brain: A work in progress (NIH Publication No. 01–4929). Retrieved September 28, 2005, from www.nimh.nih .gov/publicat/teenbrain.cfm

Nova Scotia Department of Education (1999). *Secondary science: A teaching resource.* Nova Scotia: English Program Services.

Organisation for Economic Co-operation and Development. (2004, November). *OECD Summary report on Emotions, Learning and Education.* Copenhagen, Denmark: Author.

Organisation for Economic Co-operation and Development. (2004, December). *OECD Full Report on Emotions & Learning & Education: Brain & Learning Workshop.* Copenhagen, Denmark: Author.

Ogle, D. S. (1986). *K-W-L instructional strategy* in *teaching reading as thinking.* Alexandria, VA: Association for Supervision and Curriculum Development.

Parry, T., & Gregory, G. (1998). *Designing brain-compatible learning.* Thousands Oaks, CA: Corwin Press.

Patoine, B. (2005, July/August). Peering into the brain. *BrainWork, 15*(4), 1-3.

Perkins, D. N. (1986). *Knowledge as design.* Hillsdale, NJ: Lawrence Erlbaum.

Piaget, J. (1952). *The origins of intelligence in children* (M. Cook, Trans.). New York: International Universities Press.

Radford, T. (2004, December 22). Why only dancers can do a mental pirouette. *Brain in the News, 11*(12), 1-3. (Reprinted from *The London Guardian,* p. 10, 2004, December 22)

Redenbach, S. (1984). *Color me human through true colors: Learning/personality styles to predict and understand human behavior.* Davis, CA: Esteem Seminar Programs.

Rothman, A. (2000, June 2). Alcohol damages the teen-age brain. *WebMD.* Retrieved March 21, 2007, from http://my.webmd.com/content/Article/25/1728_58212.htm

Saphier, J., & Haley, M. (1993). *Summarizers: Activity structures to support integration and retention of new learning.* Carlisle, MA: Research for Better Teaching.

Southwest Educational Developmental Laboratory. (2000). How can research on the brain inform education? *Classroom Compass, 3*(2). Retrieved March 21, 2007, from www.sedl.org/scimath/compass/v03n02/1.html

Sharan, Y., & Sharan, S. (1992). *Expanding cooperative learning through group investigations.* New York: Teachers College Press.

Smith, A. (2002). *The brain's behind it.* Stafford, Great Britain: Network Educational Press Ltd.

Sokoloff, H. (2005, May). Stress Harms Children's Memories: Montreal Study. *Brain in the News, 12*(5), 3. (Reprinted from *National Post (Canada),* p. A8, 2005, May 14)

Sousa, D. (2006). *How the brain learns* (3rd ed.). Thousand Oaks, CA: Corwin Press.

Sousa, D. (1999, February). *Brain research and student learning: New insights for educators.* Address presented at a workshop for National School Conference Institute. Phoenix, AZ: Author.

Sprenger, M. (1999). *Learning & memory: The brain in action.* Alexandria, VA: Association for Supervision and Curriculum Development.

Sternberg, R. (1985). *Beyond IQ: A triarchic theory of human intelligence.* New York: Cambridge University Press.

Strauch, B. (2003). *The primal teen: What the new discoveries about the teenage brain tell us about our kids.* New York: Anchor Books.

Sylwester, R. (1995). *A celebration of neurons: An educator's guide to the human brain.* Alexandria, VA: Association for Supervision and Curriculum Development.

Sylwester, R. (2003). *The developing adolescent brain: A complete audio workshop* [CD]. San Diego, CA: The Brain Store.

Taba, H. (1967). *Teachers' handbook for elementary social studies*. Reading, MA: Addison-Wesley.

Talukder, G. (2000, July). Decision-making is still a work in progress for teenagers. *BrainConnection.com*. Retrieved September 23, 2005, from www.brainconnection.com/topics/?main=news-in-rev/teen-frontal

Teen angst rooted in brain [Electronic version]. (2002, October 19). *NewScientist, 2365*. Retrieved March 14, 2007, from http://www.newscientist.com/article/dn2925-teen-angst-rooted-in-busy-brain.html

Torp, L., & Sage, S. (1998). *Problems as possibilities*. Alexandra, VA: Association for Supervision and Curriculum Development.

University of California, Irvine. (2004, July 20). Human intelligence determined by volume and location of gray matter tissue in brain. *ScienceDaily*. Retrieved March 14, 2007, from http://www.sciencedaily.com/releases/2004/07/040720090419.htm (Adapted from a news release issued by University of California, Irvine)

University of Cincinnati. (2005, October 10). Shift in brain's language-control site offers rehab hope; language center site becomes more lateralized with age. *ScienceDaily*. Retrieved December 23, 2005, from *http://www.sciencedaily.com/releases/2005/10/051007091742.htm* (Adapted from a news release issued by University of Cincinnati)

Vedantam, S. (2001, June 3). Are teens just wired that way? *Washington Post*, p. A01. Retrieved September 26, 2005, from www.washingtonpost.com

Verner, K. (2001). Making connections in the classroom: Brain-based learning. *Basic Education, 45*(8), 3-7.

von Glasersfeld, E. (1995). A constructivist approach to teaching. In L. P. Steffe & J. E. Gale (Eds.), *Constructivism in education*, 3-16. Hillsdale, NJ: Lawrence Erlbaum.

Vygotsky, L. S. (1978). *Mind in society: The development of higher psychological processes*. Cambridge, MA: Harvard University Press.

Wallis, C. (2004, May 10). What makes teens tick? *Time Magazine*, 42-49.

Wiggins, G., & McTighe, J. (1998). *Understanding by design*. Alexandria, VA: Association for Supervision and Curriculum Development.

Williamson, E. (2005, February 1). Brain immaturity can be deadly. *MSNBC*. Retrieved March 21, 2007, from http://www.infowars.com/articles/science/brain_immaturity_can_be_deadly.htm

Wolfe, P. (2001). *Brain matters: Translating research into classroom practice*. Alexandria, VA: Association for Supervision and Curriculum Development.

Wolfe, P., & Brandt, R. (1998, November). What do we know from brain research? *Educational Leadership, 56*(3), 8-13.

Index

Note: In page references, f indicates figures.

147

CORWIN PRESS

The Corwin Press logo—a raven striding across an open book—represents the union of courage and learning. Corwin Press is committed to improving education for all learners by publishing books and other professional development resources for those serving the field of PreK–12 education. By providing practical, hands-on materials, Corwin Press continues to carry out the promise of its motto: **"Helping Educators Do Their Work Better."**